ON LAW AND COUNTRY

*The
Biography and Speeches
of*
Russell Archibald Ramsey

By his son,
Russell Wilcox Ramsey

BRANDEN PUBLISHING CO.

© Copyright 1993
Branden Publishing Company

Library of Congress Cataloging in Publication Data

Ramsey, Russell W. (Russell Wilcox), 1935-
   On law and country : the biography and speeches of Russell Archibald Ramsey / by his son, Russell Wilcox Ramsey.
       p. cm.
   Includes bibliographical references and index.
   ISBN 0-8283-1970-7
   1. Ramsey, Russell Archibald, b. 1904.
   2. Sandusky (Ohio)--Biography.
   3. Gainsville (Fla.)--Biography.
   4. Generals--United States--Biography.
   5. United States. Army--Biography.
   I. Ramsey, Russell Archibald, b. 1904.
   II. Title.
   F499.S22R367   1993
   355'.0092--dc20   92-35979
   [B]   CIP

Branden Publishing Company
17 Station Street
Box 843 Brookline Village
Boston, MA 02147

Table of Contents

Overview 4
His People and His Region 5
The College Years 15
Marriage and the Young Lawyer 23
The World War II Years 34
1946 - 1960; the Attorney and the General 47
1961 - 1973; Community Leader & General Emeritus 57
1974 - 1992; the Gentle General 66
What Manner of Man? 76
Illustrations 80
The Speeches
    Battle for Irisan Bridge, August 1945 91
    Daughters of the American Revolution,
        September 1956 102
    Radio Station WLEC, September 1956 114
    Veteran's Day, November 1959 117
    Citizenship and the Cold War 126
    A Toast to Daniel D. White, May 1961 139
    Tribute to a War of 1812 Hero, May 1961 140
    Boy Scout Occasion, 1966 143
    Memorial Day, May 1967 150
    Pigs, October 1968 154
    Pearl Harbor Day, December 1969 164
    Tribute to Brigadier General Richard
        McNelly, 1971 172
    Memorial Day, May 1971 175
    Memorial Day, February 1974 181
    About Russell Ramsey, August 1975 186
    Exchanging-the Peace, July 1979 187
    The Gentleman, January 1991 189
Notes 190
Index 191

Overview

When he was born, gargantuan rail-mounted steam shovels were launching an attack on the muddy goop that would become the Gatun Locks of the Panama Canal. When he died, the Allied Persian Gulf Coalition Force was poised for the lightning ground, sea, and air strike that became known as Desert Storm. In the nearly eighty-seven years of life in between, Russell Archibald Ramsey exemplified two great thrusts in American history: the validity of the rule of law, and the necessity of the citizen soldier.

Underlying Russell A. Ramsey's commitment to the law and the militia were his beliefs in loyalty to family, his love of intellectual advancement, his advocacy for public service, and his practice of giving his best at each endeavor. Overarching his commitment to the law and the citizen soldiery, and sustaining the life traits that were his visible hallmarks, was a profound, unyielding faith in God, expressed through the historic and credal modes of the Episcopal Church.

His People and His Region

Gustavus F. Ramsey, son of Scottish immigrants, served the Pennsylvania Railroad in northern Ohio as telegrapher from 1872 until 1912. He and wife Margaret lived most of their years in Columbus, the capital city, and struggled hard to send their sons Raymond A. and Russell K. to Ohio State University. They were strict Methodists with an intensity magnified by the Victorian Age in which they lived. Their older son Raymond became a distinguished physician in Columbus; Russell K. studied law and, upon graduation in 1900 accepted an invitation to join the firm of King and Guerin in Sandusky. One year later, he went back to Columbus to marry his sweetheart, Florence Louise Samuel. She was petite- just barely five feet tall, never weighed a hundred pounds in her life- and known for her kindness to other people. Her father operated a well known wholesale pharmaceutical business in Columbus. She and her sisters grew up in a closely knit environment that resembled the family portrayed in Louisa May Alcott's 1868 classic *Little Women*.

Following a wedding trip in the east, Russell K. and Florence moved to Sandusky, living in two downtown apartments until the completion of their dream house, in 1905, at what is presently 1311 Columbus Avenue. Russell established himself as a leading attorney by representing such clients as the Hinde and Dauch Paper Company, Cedar Point Amusement Park, and the Wagner Quarries. The law firm worked out of upstairs offices on the west side of Columbus Avenue, just south of the old State Theater and next door to the R. M. & C. B. Wilcox Co. The ferry boats for Cedar Point, Kelley's Island, and Put-in-Bay were within easy view of these offices and were more than symbolic. Russell K. Ramsey made his reputation representing companies that plied the limestone trade, the waterfront vacation industry, and the paper carton shipping business; in fact, during his lifetime the

Hinde & Dauche Paper Company erected its landmark waterfront factory within two blocks of his office. The Third National Exchange Bank, serving many of these interests, built its downtown headquarters in 1913, a very short walk from his office, and appointed him to its Board of Directors.

Florence filled her days writing letters to her sisters, making museum quality table linens with exquisite needlework, and making friends with people from all walks of life. Once, on a visit to the Blue Hole at Castalia, she suddenly slid down the bank and dropped into the icy waters. The attraction features dark blue water that bubbles up from deep in the bowels of the earth, and was considered a bottomless pit. A bystander grabbed her hand just before the heavy, water-saturated clothes of that Victorian age would have dragged her under.

When Florence believed herself ready for the delivery of her firstborn, she went home to Columbus to stay with her oldest sister, Julia Samuel Houston. On May 11, 1904, Julia assisted Florence in a very difficult delivery- a ten pound son and a 92 pound mother- a little before midnight. The child was named Russell Archibald, the first name for his father, the middle name for his Aunt Julia's husband. Russell K. and Florence moved little Russell to their dream house when he was still an infant. A dream house it was indeed, for Russell K. built as much structure as he could afford to resemble a splendid house in Columbus that his brother-in-law Archibald Houston had built for Florence's sister, Julia.

His Boyhood Years

Columbus Avenue, in the early 1900s, led to the Sandusky Fairgrounds, site of the racetrack described in Sherwood Anderson's charming tale "I'm a Fool." South of Scott Street, the avenue was still on the outer rim of town, but stately new two-story homes were being built well back from the street, and a grass clad boulevard was left between the public sidewalk and the curbstone, resulting in deep front lawns. As an adult, Russell did not often reminisce about his boyhood years, but when he did, he shared solid recollections with loving care.

He was enrolled at Campbell School, just a block behind his family house, and his first grade teacher was the redoubtable Miss Emmeline Baumeister, later Principal and then Supervisor of Elementary Instruction for the district. On Saturday afternoons at home he would sit on the stone steps, watching the traffic on the sidewalk and Columbus Avenue. Old men in dark blue jackets, with tattered medals pinned to the lapel, would pass by. These were Civil War veterans who lived at the Ohio Soldiers' and Sailors' Home on South Columbus Avenue. On Saturdays, they would take their small allowance and walk four miles to dingy bars on Water Street near Sandusky Bay, drink up their cash, and stumble homeward.

"Class," said his second grade teacher, "what are soldiers, and what do they do?"

Young Russell's hand shot up. "I know!" he asserted. He got to his feet, walked to the front of the class, and began staggering and stumbling across the front of the room. "This," he announced in triumph, "is what soldiers do!"

The teacher was horrified and sent him to the Principal's office. The public schools in 1912 were more interested in decorum than in academic precision. Thirty-two years later, as Ohio's 37th National Guard Division drove into the outskirts of

Manila, Colonel Russell A. Ramsey gave orders to have hot, thirsty soldiers stopped from drinking the beer at the newly liberated San Miguel Brewery. The beer was still green, and it would give the men violent attacks of diarrhea.

Russell K. gave his son a "BB" gun in 1912, over his mother's strong opposition. One hot summer day, a German immigrant woman employed as the laundress was in the back yard hanging up clothes to dry. Young Russell sat on the front steps with his "BB" gun. The trash man's cart hove into view on Columbus Avenue, pulled by a stout draft horse. Russell watched in fascination as the cart pulled to the curb and stopped. The trash man dismounted, seized a bucket of trash, and threw it atop his wagon. Russell drew a bead on the horse's rear end across the top of his sights, just as the manual said to do, and squeezed off a perfect shot. The horse reared up, then bolted southward on Columbus Avenue with the trash man in hot pursuit. In a burst of speed he overtook the surprised animal, reigned him to a halt, then walked horse and cart back to the curb in front of the Ramsey house.

"Where ees ze boy who done thees?" he growled in a thick Italian accent. Young Russell raced down the driveway into the back yard, darted behind the laundress, and crouched down, hiding himself in her thick layers of ankle length skirt.

"Vot boy iss you looking for?" she asked the infuriated Italian in her German accent.

"Zee boy who shoota my horse!" he roared, peering behind her but not daring to touch her.

Russell's heart beat loudly as his assailant glared menacingly, then finally gave up and stomped back to his horse and wagon. Thirty-three years later in northern Luzon, of the Philippines, Russell squeezed off one well aimed shot with a U.S. Army .45 caliber pistol, dropping a Japanese Imperial Army lieutenant who was just three steps away from decapitating him with a Samurai sword.

Florence took her young son downtown shopping one day in 1911 to the R.M. & C.B. Wilcox Co., after visiting her husband at his office next door. Her venue was the "R.M. & C.B. Wilcox Co.," a clothing store managed by Merritt S. Wilcox (son of " R. M. ") who was also her neighbor half a block to the south on Columbus Avenue. Merritt spoke graciously to her, and then pointed out that his own son, Richard, whom she knew from the neighborhood, was there to help out a bit. Russell and Richard thus became best friends, both through visiting their fathers' offices, and in the neighborhood. Later, Merritt and Janet Wilcox moved to a house on W. Adams Street, meaning that young Richard would attend Monroe School instead of Campbell. However, Richard and Russell joined the same Boy Scout troop and went on several hikes together. They also exchanged spend-the-night outings at each others' homes. The only thing that occasionally interfered with their fun was the inconvenience of Richard's little sister, Louise, who was five years younger than the two adventurous boys. To Louise Wilcox, Russell A. Ramsey was just another pig-headed boy who ran around with her big brother.

In late summer of 1913, Florence S. Ramsey contracted a kidney infection of a sort that today is cured with one course of pills, following an out-patient visit or two to the physician's office. Doctors and family members spoke darkly, too, of damage inflicted to her kidneys when her petite body was delivering young Russell, a strapping baby. Her condition worsened, and the distraught Russell K. arranged for her to be put aboard a special train car in Sandusky, thence to be transported to a leading hospital in Columbus recommended by his physician brother, Dr. Raymond Ramsey. The Sandusky newspaper ran plaintive stories about Florence's courageous six week battle for life. But the day came in mid September when Russell K. had to tell his son that his beloved mother was dead. The funeral and burial were in Columbus. Young Russell, in the code of Victorian manhood, put his grief into a secret shrine known only to him and to his God. He put the tender memories of his mother into his innermost being and, for the rest of his life, he would never share more than tiny anecdotes about her. His feelings, his adoration, the joyous mother-son relationship that had been theirs- all this was buried in a mountain of grief that could not be expressed in that age when ex-President Teddy Roosevelt trumpeted manhood and bravery to the youth of America.

Russell K. took his son on a trek that was intended to heal their grief and strengthen their father-son bonds. For seven days the saddened boy sat on train cars, riding through the great west and watching for buffalo who never revealed themselves, perhaps having grown wary of the fifty cents-per-crack gunmen who rode on trains in that era for the thrill of watching a running buffalo fall as you squeezed off a rifle shot. Seventy-eight years later, with his memory failing, Russell patted a buffalo's face at the Albany, Georgia zoo, reaching through the fence from his seat in a wheelchair.

"They never would come out where you could see them on my trip," his struggling mind recalled. "My father kept saying there would be buffalo to see."

The healing trip nearly became a tragedy in itself. Russell K. was of the Edwardian mode in the exercise of fatherhood, sternly but lovingly preparing and teaching his boy to be a success in the world. When young Russell needed to hear that his father still loved him, and that God would take care of his mother in Heaven, instead he was grilled on naming all the state capitals as the train thundered westward. When they arrived in San Francisco, young Russell caught a bad case of scarlet fever and barely survived. Twenty-nine years later, Major Russell A. Ramsey organized entertainment for the 18,500 men of Ohio's 37th Division in San Francisco while they awaited shipment to the Pacific Theater. Among the film stars who volunteered their services was a young actor named Ronald Reagan, who impressed Major Ramsey with his sincere desire to please these wartime citizen soldiers from Ohio.

Russell K. and Russell A. returned to Sandusky, well into the fall, and their world would never be the same again. Oh, there were still a few laughs. Once, Russell K. was trying to help his son launch a kite, right in the boulevard in front of the house on Columbus Avenue. Sternly, he lectured his son on the importance of holding the kite at the correct angle while you ran with it. In his three-piece suit with high starched collar, he ran briskly across the yard with the kite, watching his son hold the string and calling out instructions. He caught his foot on the iron service head of the gas main which stuck up through the lawn, falling hard and rolling over several times. Young Russell laughed until tears streamed from his eyes.

But Russell K. was not adept at making a home for a young boy. His concept of being a father and head of family would fit beautifully into the British Broadcasting System's 1971 screen portrayal of *The Forsyte Saga*, adapted from John Galsworthy's novel trilogy. So he found things wanting at Campbell School and, perhaps under the pretext of educational deficiencies, told his son that it was time to go to a fine preparatory school. The one selected was Howe Military School, operated near Angola, Indiana by the Episcopal Church. The program was a meld of British boarding school and stern military regimen, with Episcopalian high church training and worship services. The campus featured Gothic British architecture and beautiful stretches of green lawn in season. Russell attended Howe for his second and third grade years of school, doing remarkably well for a boy who had just lost his mother and nearly died from scarlet fever. But his father's life was changing, too.

First, W.E. Guerin, senior partner of his law firm, moved to Oregon. The firm would pass through several evolutions of partnerships, embracing such illustrious Sandusky legal names as Roy H. Williams, George C. Steinemann, Edmund B. King, and Joseph Pyle. Second, he fell in love with Helen Wilcox, daughter of C. B. Wilcox, an owning partner in the dry goods store next door to his law office. Third, he missed his son, away at Howe School. Fourth, his star was rising in Sandusky affairs: Directorship in the Sandusky Business Men's Association, President of the prestigious Sunyendeand Club, high office in both branches of the Masonic Order, Junior and later Senior Warden of Grace Episcopal Church, and an officer in the Sandusky Commercial

Federation. All these things were to bring him a new family situation, great honor in his community, and, inevitably, personal conflict.

In June, 1915, Russell K. married Helen Wilcox at Grace Episcopal Church. Helen set about to bring a woman's touch to the Ramsey home at 1311 Columbus Avenue. Despite the difficulty of coming in just two years after the death of the beloved and revered Florence, she set up a warm, delightful relationship with her new stepson that would endure until her death in 1967. Young Russell was taken out of Howe Military School and resumed attendance at Campbell School. He joined the Boy Scouts with his pal Richard Wilcox, who was a second cousin (grandson of "R.M." Wilcox) of his new stepmother. He sang soprano for a while as a Grace Church Chorister. And world events touched his life in 1917, his ninth grade year, in powerful ways.

Russell K. had been designated Chairman of the Liberty Bond Committee, a component of the country's emergency system for meeting the unaccustomed financial demands of mobilization during World War I. His sales efforts on all five national bond drives were extremely successful, and, when the first contingent of Sandusky troops marched off for Army induction, Russell was selected to give a rousing speech at the train station. He was suffering from laryngitis, but he threw himself into the project enthusiastically.

"One hundred citizens of this community are leaving to join their compatriots in the ranks of the citizen soldiery of the republic. Just as the few hundreds of patriots in the days of the colonists laid aside the implements of the farm, of the factory, the workshop and the store and took up arms to oppose the injustice and tyranny of the government of the mother country, so you men, my fellow citizens, have laid aside your peaceful occupations to fight for the principles which gave your country birth. (...) So, when the dark clouds of this world war shall have passed down beyond the horizon and the bright sun of peace shall shine once more, the final victory will have been a world triumph won by the same fiber of citizen-soldiers for those same principles of democracy in which our great nation was conceived. (...) The days of Prussian militarism are numbered, and there is in the ascendancy the star of the citizen soldier fighting for humanity, for equality among men, for the prevention of military aggression with its horrible atrocities committed upon the inhabitants of weak prostrate nations. (...) You have been called upon to help bear the brunt and to provide the answer to those who dare say that sons of Ohio will be found lacking in their full duty!"

Russell K. died in 1932, never knowing that the son who bore his name would rise to high rank in the Ohio National Guard and earn multiple decorations for bravery in battle against another militaristic aggressor. In 1918, with World War I approaching its climax, he decided to send his son back to Howe Military School for the final three years of high school. Years later, his son would talk about the weak leadership and the rowdy student behavior that were rampant at Sandusky High School during that era. So, whether for reasons patriotic or academic, young Russell again became a military cadet. His father and Helen made the adventurous overland drive to north-central Indiana in their Cadillac touring sedan several times to visit him.

Russell's final three years at Howe provided him with the environment in which to show what his intellect, his drive, and his iron self-discipline could do for a boy. His mother's petite size meant that his body would mature at a wiry five feet, eight inches in height; it was a stature that enabled him to become a star on the high bar in gymnastics. His love of the Episcopal Church and its liturgy led him to become an acolyte, performing the rituals of each service with loving precision in the Cadet Chapel that looked like a Gothic English church. His grades were nearly perfect, and he demonstrated an intellectual hunger that caused his teachers to insist to his father that he must attend one of the finest colleges in the land.

Each year, Howe Military School sponsored an elocution contest; winners at each level were awarded a medal of genuine silver. During both his junior and senior year, he won the upper division with flawless presentations, from memory, of Edward E. Hale's 1823 classic novelette *The Man Without A Country*. While the perfect elocution of eighty pages before a group of judges was a feat of memory, the content of the story- a U.S. officer's loss of contact with his country as punishment for an act of rebellion- drilled patriotism into Russell's being, an active, reasoned patriotism that would manifest itself all his life.

In his junior year at Howe, he was Cadet First Sergeant of Company "B"; in the 1940s he could still call company roll from memory. In his senior year he was Cadet 1st Lieutenant, in the post of Battalion Adjutant. This is the showy job at cadet parades, the person who calls the units to attention, receives the "All Present" report, faces the Cadet First Captain, and renders the status report with a smart saber salute. In late 1990, with just a few weeks yet to live and his brain reeling under multiple ischemiatic attacks, he could still name the cadet officers at Howe Military School from their photograph in the 1921 yearbook.

Russell K. and Helen acquired a choice lot on a bluff overlooking Lake Erie, about two miles east of Huron on the Cleveland Road (U.S. Routes 2 and 6) and erected a wooden cottage. The Lake Shore Electric Co. ran an inter-urban car, in those days, from downtown Sandusky, just two doors from Russell K.'s office, all the way to Cleveland. The driver would stop the car right in front of the lake cottage. Following the eleven mile electric rail trek from Huron to Sandusky, one could take a local car from the downtown station to the house at 1311 Columbus Avenue. So they could actually commute from the remote lake shore cottage more conveniently than many people in the 1990s can get to work from downtown residences.

The College Years

In the fall of 1921, young Russell boarded the New York Central train at the Sandusky station and headed eastward for Princeton University. His parents made continuous improvements on the Huron house during his college years, increasing their residence there during the warm months. Russell K. added a stable and bought several riding horses. He, Helen, and their son all became excellent equestrians. The lake front property included a farm on the south side of the Cleveland Road, within walking distance of the lake house. Russell K. rented the farm portion of his estate to an expert farmer, driving the poor man to distraction with his scientific schemes for pig breeding, crop selection, and other technical matters on which he read books but had no practical knowledge.

At Princeton, young Russell brought continuous pride to the family. In those days, top American universities followed the British curriculum model; one studied mathematics, the sciences, history, languages, literature, and social sciences. There was no majoring in this or that- the goal was simply to produce educated people who could then specialize through additional training.

Russell enrolled in Army Reserve Officers Training Corps, as his father before him had done at Ohio State in the 1890s. The cadets were formed into two horse-drawn artillery batteries. He worked hard at horsemanship and tried out for a slot on the polo team, which competed in intercollegiate circles but was sponsored by the Army ROTC detachment. He won a spot on the first team, in the number one "attack" position, and led Princeton's poloists to several winning seasons. His biggest thrill was scoring the winning goal to defeat Army in the West Point Riding Hall in 1924.

Russell tried out briefly for football, his freshman year, but was far too light. A big varsity lineman ended his career in the second practice by breaking his nose painfully during a violent blocking assignment. At gymnastics, however, he was a solid varsity performer, winning a letter and competing against the Ivy League teams. Once, a manager forgot to dry off and apply talcum powder to the high bar. Russell attempted the full somersault on the flyaway dismount, failed to complete the 360 degree rotation on the sticky bar, and plowed into the mat, nose first. It was the second major break in three years and left his nose with a prominently arched profile.

Russell had an English professor who despised modernism in literature and shamelessly extolled the works of Alfred, Lord Tennyson and the romantics. Throughout his life, when a friend was vexed with a personal dilemma, Russell would quote from "Idylls of the King": "More things are wrought by prayer than this world dreams of."

Helen and Russell K. hoped for a child of their own but were unable to conceive. They wrote to a reputable adoption agency and were put in touch with an orphanage that had a delightful, bright, and pretty girl who needed a home. They named her Jean, and she was a lucky child, indeed, for Russell K. and Helen each had their own reasons for needing such a daughter in their lives. Her ready made big brother and she became instant best pals; Russell taught her to ride horses in the approved polo form. And Jean filled an emotional void in his life that grew out of the tragic early loss of his mother, and the well intended but ever stern mannerisms of his father.

In his senior year, Russell took the family dog Mack to college with him. Mack was a bull terrier who had embarrassed Russell K. by dog fighting with the pooches of several family friends, even killing the family pet of a friends on Wayne Street. But Mack attended classes in a most gentlemanly fashion throughout young Russell's senior year. Once he raised howls of laughter in the lecture hall by standing up to yawn and stretch ostentatiously as the professor droned into the repeat telling of a boring anecdote. Russell signed up for an honors section in astronomy, in his senior year, finding quickly that the course conflicted with his ROTC work and interested him little. He sought to drop the course and substitute another.

"I'll let you out of this course, Ramsey, if you can solve this problem," growled the doughty old professor. He handed Russell a seemingly impossible requirement to determine the distance between two celestial bodies under certain conditions. Quickly, Russell determined that the calculations were endless and would literally fill his semester. He jumped aboard a local train for New York City and went to see a banker friend.

"We have a new machine," said his friend. "It's called a digital calculator. It runs off lengthy calculations in seconds that would take days and days. Some day," added the friend, "they will figure out how to run these things with electricity." Quickly they ran off the many calculations, and, the next morning Russell entered the astronomy professor's office with one long number, written on a scrap of paper. The professor smirked, acting out a little scenario in which many students had been humiliated before. Slowly he opened a desk drawer, fished out some papers, and compared Russell's answer with his own calculation.

" My God, Ramsey," he burst out. "Congratulations! You have it right. You're the first one ever. How'd you do it?" Quickly Russell filled the professor in on the wonders of digital computers, but his senior year was filled with bigger issues. Selected to graduate cum laude, and holding one of the two cadet captaincies in the Army R.O.T.C. unit, he was tendered a Regular Army, active duty commission for June of 1925, with a serial number to rank just behind the graduating class at West Point. He was also accepted to Ohio State University's Law College, where his father was an alumnus. And he had fine job offers in New York City, where the financial community was acting out the "Roaring Twenties" boom. It was clearly a watershed time in his life, and in early spring he came home for a week to ponder.

Sandusky, in those days, had a resident unit of the U.S. Army Corps of Engineers. It was headed by a captain, who agreed to take Russell to lunch and talk about Army careers.

"You'll notice I'm only a captain, and I'm not a young man," said this forthright officer. "The country is negotiating an international peace treaty (eventually the Paris Treaty Outlawing War of 1928, and the London Naval Disarmament Treaty of 1930). "There's talk of offering West Point and Annapolis graduates the right to accept their diplomas and go directly into the Reserve, without ever serving on active duty. Your father is a prominent attorney here, and I'd think you would do well to go on to law school."

Russell's father and Helen drove all the way to Princeton a few weeks later for his graduation, a big adventure for that time, and Russell basked in family pride. His little sister Jean had nothing but wide eyed admiration for her handsome big brother in an officer's uniform with a Sam Browne belt dashingly across one shoulder.

But he decided to try Army life anyway, for a time, reporting to Camp Sacket Harbor near Watertown, New York to participate in a shabbily funded program called the Officers Reserve Corps. He excelled in every way and felt a strong calling to be integrated into the Regular Army when the training stint ended. But the Engineer Corps captain's words haunted him, and his father was now pressuring him directly to pursue a legal career. And so he did, but it was not to be smooth sailing.

In the fall of 1925, Russell matriculated at Ohio State Law College, and his father's heart was bursting with pride. The freshmen, in that era, were required to join the law fraternity, and that fraternity was part of a disgraceful national pattern of destructive hazing and pranks, a fact often overlooked in rosy-- tinted remembrances of the "Roaring Twenties." Specifically, the freshmen were required, at Thanksgiving, to steal a turkey from a blind man who ran a food store near the campus. The prizes from this exploit were roasted and served amid a climate of great mirth, and no one worried much about what happened at the home of the victimized merchant. For the organization catering to the neophyte guardians of American law in Ohio, and clearly

Ohio State's law graduates dominated both law and politics in that era, it was a morally indefensible situation.

Russell served notice to the pledge committee that he would not comply with the requirement to steal the turkey.

"Then you'll never get in the law fraternity, Ramsey," jeered the upper classmen.

Russell took his case to the Dean. "May I attend the Law College, get my degree, and not join the fraternity?" he asked. "I do not believe the turkey stealing tradition is right."

"Aw, come on, Ramsey, the men are just having a little fun," rationalized the Dean. "Truth is, our men always give that Italian fellow some money- it's just a little game. He probably doesn't even care. Be a sport! Think of your legal career, and your future relationship with your colleagues."

Russell took the Dean's advice literally. Despite his father's mixed enthusiasm for a moral decision of idealistic youth, Russell withdrew from Ohio State and matriculated at rival Michigan Law College in Ann Arbor.

"You'll never practice law in Ohio, Ramsey," the law fraternity men told him when he was packing up his things to leave. "Michigan law is different. You won't pass the Ohio State Bar Exam, and no Ohio lawyer will ever cooperate with you on a case. Believe it!"

So Russell went to Michigan with a special burden, a special commitment in his heart. Perhaps his study there had a certain intensity that made his faculty wonder what force was driving him, and his grades were superb.

On one football weekend, Russell K. and Helen drove up to Ann Arbor in a big touring Cadillac to visit their son and see the game. Russell was in the right front seat while his father drove him across Ann Arbor to pick up Helen and Russell's date for dinner. A cold, driving rain had set in, and cars were not as safe then as now. The road suddenly came to an end, and there was a barrier of saw horses. The brakes failed, and the big car plunged into a deep ditch, slamming against an embankment. Russell K. was badly shaken up. His son had a deep cut, made by a piece of windshield glass, from the lower edge of his left eyelid, running over two inches down his cheek, leaving a scar that would remain for life. That his eye survived was a miracle.

Russell's summers during the Michigan Law College years were taken up at the family beach home with horseback riding, doing things with Jean, working on his father's farm across the highway, and reading some law in his father's office. His uncle, Dr. Raymond Ramsey, had bought a summer cottage at Chaska Beach, a mile west from his family lake house and nearer to the village of Huron. There, he and Jean deepened friendships with their first cousins William, Robert, and Norman Ramsey. And Russell's commitment to being a militia officer took an unexpected turn.

Each summer, during the Michigan years, he would receive orders for two weeks of military duty at Ft. Knox, then the Cavalry School of the Regular Army. But no duty assignment ever appeared in the orders. The reason became apparent in June, 1926.

Ft. Knox, the Cavalry School, had an annual grudge match on the polo field against Ft. Sill, the Army Artillery School. Cannons were still horse-drawn in 1926, and Army Artillery horsemen were as numerous as cavalrymen, who were seen by some as part of a dying branch of warfare. The Commandant of the Artillery School scouted out the awesome young polo player, 2d Lt. Russell A. Ramsey, who was to perform summer training, and had him placed on special duty with the Artillery Polo Team. In Russell's third year of these fiercely contested matches, the Commandant of the Cavalry School decided to take the field personally and lead his men to victory.

"Be careful, lieutenant," the stable sergeant briefed young Russell. "No one pushes the general too hard- he's supposed to look good out there."

The idealistic young Reservist thought about whether he wanted to make a Regular Army general look good on the polo field by cutting him some slack. But the sergeant had more.

"And lieutenant- " he cut in. "That horse you're on- he's trained as a crowder."

Russell knew quite well that a "crowder" in polo was a horse trained to dig in his feet, upon a knee command from the rider, and literally push the nearest horse sideways. The "crowder" horse probably did not know that the rider would only give the knee signal when a key opponent's horse was riding too close to the little wooden wall that defines the outlines of a polo field. The maneuver was designed, when it worked right, to spill the opposing horse and rider, leaving the rider of the "crowder" horse free to steal the ball and drive goalward.

Russell played the game to win, and the Artillerymen were one goal ahead with seconds left in the game. Then, the Cavalry General got the ball and thundered down the outside of the field, his horse's hooves within inches of the wooden wall. Russell went on defense, the last rider left to prevent the score, and drove right up on the General's horse. Instinctively, he drove his knee into his mount for closer position. The loyal horse did his best, digging his feet into the Kentucky turf and heaving the other horse with all his might. The General and his horse went over the fence; the horse fell, and the General, fortunately for his personal safety, was thrown clear. A huge melee of players and officials now entered the field.

"Ramsey, go out, I'm replacing you," said the Artillery team captain tersely.

Russell trotted his horse over to the Artillery sidelines, where the stable sergeant grabbed his horse's reins.

"Lieutenant," he said, "my instructions are to tell you to get off that horse, and to get your ass out of Ft. Knox on the next train. I warned you!"

It would be Russell's last polo episode as a Reservist, and it served to open his eyes to two things: the ugly politics that existed between the Regular Army and the Reserve components, and the simple fact that the Reserve, with the exception of a few National Guard units, which were under state control, had no real military task nor organization. Each of these experiences became stored somewhere within his being, and he would act upon them with power and substance when leadership opportunities opened before him.

Russell graduated in early Jane, 1928, from Michigan Law College, earning the Bachelor of Law (L.L.B., changed in 1967 to the Doctor Juris, or J.D.) with honors. His faculty encouraged him to stay on and study for the Master of Law (L.L.M.) degree, but this was primarily for professors who would become careerists in academic law. He loved the intellectual side of legal study, and there is little doubt that he would have made a great law professor, given his later skill in showing people how government is supposed to work during hundreds of speeches for public events. But his father pointed out that academic law is not always "real law," and Russell now found that two very large forces were calling him. He was at the age when young men of that era thought about settling down with a family, and his father talked often of practicing law with his son.

Marriage and the Young Lawyer

During his summers, while reading some law at his father's office, he noticed that the younger sister of his old pal Richard Wilcox was now grown up, beautiful beyond description, and working for her father at the R.M. and C.B. Wilcox store next door. Richard had already finished college and moved to New York; Louise, his once pestiferous little sister, was now the raving beauty that people in Sandusky talked about. She had attended two years of college in Boston and then went to work for her father, Merritt Wilcox (son of "R.M." Wilcox), who managed the store. Making the romance interesting was the fact that Louise was the second cousin of Russell's stepmother Helen, who was the daughter of "C.B." Wilcox, nephew of "R.M." and president of the company. Russell spent the months from June, 1928 until March, 1929 as an associate in his father's law office. While he gave some genuine help on cases, he used the time to read Ohio case law, which was more different from Michigan case law than it is today, remembering the dire predictions that he could not pass the Ohio Bar Exam.

Russell and Louise had wonderful, romantic times at the family lake house. Once, they went cantering down the beach on horseback, pulling up suddenly for a private moment in a secluded spot. Suddenly, Louise lost her balance and started to slip out of the saddle. Russell reached out in a dashing gesture to stabilize his lady love, grabbed her white blouse, and pulled it right off her body, leaving her atop her mount in her bra.

In July, 1928, Russell took the Ohio Bar exam. Six weeks later, he suffered the crushing blow of receiving a notice, by mail, that he had failed. Now he and his father wondered if Michigan law preparation really was so vastly different from Ohio law, or if, perhaps, the turkey stealing affair at the Ohio State University law fraternity had truly resulted in partisan retribution by dishonest exam readers.

Frantically he boned up on Ohio law for several weeks and took the exam again. This time, he was notified that he had passed in the number one spot, a tribute both to Russell's legal knowledge and, let it be said, to the integrity of the Ohio Bar Examiners who apparently did not, when push came to shove, retaliate over the turkey affair in 1925. A hilarious sideshow to this traumatic experience took place when a Columbus newspaper, seeing Russell's "Rural Free Delivery (RFD)" address in Huron, headlined the bar exam results with "Farmer Boy From Huron First in Bar Exam."

On June 8, 1929, Louise and Russell were married in Grace Episcopal Church, with a reception at Plum Brook Country Club. Bride and groom brought in their college roommates as maid of honor and best man, and as bridesmaids and ushers. There was much collegiate cutting up at the rehearsal and the reception, for this was the moment in American history that no one could see coming at the time, the apex before the crash on the Roaring Twenties. Even the relatively broad minded old Sandusky Episcopalians were shocked when the hit song "Ah, Sweeet Mystery of Life" was played at the wedding, and it was the last secular music ever played in Grace Church. Russell K. and Helen had moved to the lake house, and Russell and Louise now moved into the family residence at 1311 Columbus Avenue in Sandusky. Their wedding trip to Yama Farms, New York would serve for a nostalgic film on the 1920s.

It was the custom, each night at that elegant resort, for the newest married couple to be presented grandly at a formal ball. All the guests were in tails and ballroom gowns, and the live orchestra played the Broadway hit tunes of the day. On their first night, Russell discovered that he had no belt for his dress black trousers. He borrowed one of his bride's narrow black dress belts to hold his pants up discreetly under the formal cutaway coat. Louise dressed up in a gorgeous ball gown that would have gained her a film tryout in Hollywood. The quests formed a semi-circle at the base of the wide, sweeping staircase. The music was muted, a soft drumroll began, and the hostess began reading a little biographical introduction of her newest honeymooner couple. Russell and Louise appeared at the head of the first flight of stairs, on a wide landing, awaiting the signal.

The hostess gave her signal. Russell was to descend first to the bottom, then turn grandly and look up the stairs as his radiantly beautiful bride came down to join him. He started forward, and his right toe slipped under a raised edge in the thick rug at the head of the stairs. On his next step, he lost his balance, pitched forward, and rolled head over heels in formal regalia to the bottom of the stairs.

The guests cried out in concern, and Louise ran down the stairs to see about her fallen husband. The hostess regained control by asking him ostentatiously if he had hurt himself. He shook his head in humiliated silence. Twenty-six years later, he stepped on the loose lid of a sewer manhole in front of the Erie County Court House en route to his office, falling part way into the hole and injuring his knee painfully. A gentleman who owed him some money from an unpaid legal bill rushed up and crowed in an obsequious manner for others to hear, "Oh, General Ramsey, did you hurt yourself?"

"Why, Hell no," he barked. "I do this every morning for exercise!" Perhaps he would have liked to say the same thing at Yama Farms, on his wedding trip.

The newlyweds took up residence on Columbus Avenue in a climate of delirious happiness. Then, the events unfolded that make married life and careers a reality, but Louise and Russell would always retain warm, romantic memories for those giddy days in 1929 when their love was new and America was rose tinted.

Five months after their wedding, the New York Stock Exchange crashed. Lives were ruined in Sandusky within a few days. Fortunately, the major business enterprises which sustained the law firm now known as King, Flynn, Ramsey, and Pyle mostly survived. One prominent businessman in Sandusky took his own life by leaping out the window at the Sunyendeand Club; several others quietly left town. Russell K. had invested his earnings in stocks, to some degree, which took huge losses; but he also held interests in solid companies that still produced, and in property that would rise again in value when the crisis passed. So he was never ruined, and his son was able to continue earning a salary from the law firm.

On November 23, 1930, Louise presented Russell at Good Samaritan Hospital with a beautiful daughter. She was named Florence Louise, for her paternal grandmother who died so cruelly young in 1913, and her mother. For a year, Russell and Louise gloried in taking their beautiful, precocious little girl to visit "Hellie, Jeanie, and Grampy Ramsey" at the lake house, to see Merritt and Janet Wilcox, who were soon to be retitled "Oh-oh and Pop," the "Oh-oh" stemming from the fact that Janet Wilcox would sing little songs to the lyrics "Oh-oh, oh." Life was still wondrous, even if the economy was a serious problem.

In 1931, Russell K. began having lower back pains and fevers. A kidney disease was diagnosed; again, as in the case of his first wife, it was a condition that today would be cured in non-remarkable fashion. His health deteriorated fast, and home care nurses from Sandusky were brought out to the Huron house by streetcar to work twelve hour shifts at the unheard of rate of $7 per day. Just as little Florence, now called "Floss" by the family, was making big friends with Grampy Ramsey, his illness became terminal. He died on February 20, 1932 and was interred at Woodlawn Cemetery in Sandusky, apart from his first wife Florence, who was buried in Columbus.

Russell's life was changed by the death of his father. For a time, he remained with his father's firm; but the lawyers were older men of another generation, old friends of his deceased father. His Army Reserve service was unsatisfactory. Oh- they had promoted him to 1st lieutenant, an almost embarrassing situation for him to accept because he did no real training, and yet he believed devoutly in the system.

When little Floss was a toddler, Russell decided to switch from the Officers Reserve Corps to the Ohio National Guard, a decision that would radically influence his life. While the Ramsey men were staunch Republicans, the election of Franklin D. Roosevelt to the White House brought a major change in the U.S. militia system that worked out heavily in Russell's favor. The Army and Navy Reserves, which were just paper mobilization rosters, were given some units and some missions. The Army National Guard, a holdover from the old colonial and early state militia system, was not performing well, and yet Americans still favored some kind of state retention of control over the militia. The problem was that, while the National Guard units were under state control, in peacetime, the forty-eight governors often filled their officer ranks with unqualified political appointees who did little real training.

President Roosevelt's solution, perhaps the only F.D.R. decision that earned approval in the Ramsey house back then, was to impose federal training, commissioning, and pay standards on the National Guard, but leave the units under state control except when federalized in time of national emergency.

Battery "E" of the 135th Artillery, 37th Infantry Division was a desultory guard unit in Sandusky, housed in a building with great jagged roof panels near Battery Park, the municipal docking and recreation facility. Russell applied for a commission in the unit, when it became federally recognized in 1933, and was accepted. The price was high; he was demoted to 2d lieutenant. But the three existing officers in the unit failed to qualify for federal commissions and were removed. Russell became Battery Commander and was promoted to 1st lieutenant. His situation was uncomfortable during the switch from state to federally-recognized status, for the old state National Guard officers remained in command for a few weeks while Russell, the junior officer in the battery, was forced to sign for all the property because he held the only federally recognized commission. Many items were missing, and training was highly unprofessional.

Somehow, he surmounted this delicate situation without creating enemies who would haunt him later.

Russell now began to duplicate his father's rise to regional leadership. He was selected as Junior Warden at Grace Episcopal Church. His National Guard Battery performed well in training and was soon being requested by high state officials for public ceremonies which they often found it convenient to perform during the Lake Erie beach and boating season. He served a term as President of the Junior Chamber of Commerce, and, more significantly for those Great Depression years, headed the Community Chest Fund Drive in 1934 and 1935. The community wisdom was that, since Russell K. could sell War Bonds in 1917 and 1918, Russell A. could raise money to support the local hospitals, charitable agencies, and social services during the worst two economic years in the region's modern history. It was tough going, but his volunteer organization, the forerunner of today's United Way, exceeded the budgetary goal in both years. His success led to appointment to the Board of Directors of Good Samaritan Hospital, a post he would hold, minus the war years, for the next thirty-five years.

On May 29, 1935, his beloved "Louie" presented him with a son, who became the third Russell in the sequence. His middle name Wilcox honored Louise's family. Sandusky, in that era, had recent immigrants who hired on as domestics. They were Germans, Austrians, Irish, and Italians, many fleeing the economic hard times plus the Fascists and Nazis on the European Continent. There was also a population of African-Americans, many of them immigrants from the deep south, recruited during World War I to work in the steel factories. Russell and Louise were able to have a full-time house maid, who had her own bedroom upstairs; a yard man for the warm months who also shoveled snow in winter; a laundress who came once weekly; and, for the infant months of both children, a nurse.

Russell formed his own law firm with another young attorney named Clyde Patterson. The firm took few "walk-in" clients; their services were on annual retainer by blue chip

Sandusky businesses like the Wagner Quarries, the Esmond Dairy, and the Western Security Bank. Always, Russell operated by his father's legal dictum: keep the client out of court. This principle contained no cynicism at all; in fact, it contained its own code of ethics that could cost Russell a good paying client. It meant that a corporate attorney saw to it that his clients only did things that were fully legal, so that, when challenged in a suit, the attorney had only to present the correct and prevailing case law to win. He served once on a team of lawyers who argued a case before the U.S. Supreme Court in Washington D.C., and he helped change a miserably unfair Ohio consumer law.

Once, a judge asked Russell to defend an accused murderer, the *pro bono* service that lawyers were expected to render in the days before counties had public defenders. He took the case, felt terrible about it, but gave it his best. The client was a woman who stood accused of killing her husband. Feeling that a jury would not sympathize with the doctrine of "reasonable doubt," he requested a panel of three judges in lieu of jury. He won acquittal for the woman with brilliant work in an unaccustomed field, and wondered afterwards if he had done the right thing. It would be the first and only criminal case of his career.

As war clouds loomed over Europe, in the late 1930s, Russell's family was becoming more complicated. His step--mother Helen married the amiable Ted Harten. The couple decided to live at the Huron lake house in summer, and in Fort Myers, Florida during the cold months. Their daughter Jean was now achieving brilliantly in college but still loved her summers at home in the beach house, and horseback riding with her mother Helen and her new step-father Ted.

The R.M. & C.B. Wilcox store had failed financially by 1929, a victim of chain store marketing advantages. In an era before Social Security, Merritt and Janet were left with meager savings and no income whatsoever. They sold their family house on Adams Street and bought a gray bungalow at 2136 Columbus Avenue. Merritt Wilcox tried with little success, in the Depression, to sell life insurance; Janet studied early American decorating and began selling magnificently painted trays, chairs, and wastebaskets. A sign by the door proclaimed "Wee House Antiques." Yet while the Depression was still in progress, Merritt suffered a massive heart attack and other health troubles, leaving the aging couple dependent on Janet's sometime earnings. Russell and Louise, and Louise's brother Richard, now married to the gracious Lois Zimmerman and serving as a bank officer in New York, had to supplement their income.

Young Floss loved her visits to both pairs of grandparents, and she attended Campbell School, where "Miss Emmeline," her father's onetime teacher, was now the Principal. Academically gifted, Floss skipped the second grade and was a great challenge to teachers, who had to find books that she had not yet read.

While Russell's Battery "E" was well trained, the lack of budgetary support for both the Regular Army and the Reserve forces, in the late 1930s, resulted in comic opera situations that must have given encouragement to leaders like Hitler and Mussolini in Europe. The battery's guns were still World War I pieces, French made 75 millimeter equipment, plus some early 105 mm howitzers which had to be towed with Ford station wagons that seldom ran well and could not traverse off-the-road terrain.

Promoted to captain in 1938, Russell had his hands full when his unit took the field. Once, the toll collector on the Bay Bridge across the base of Sandusky Bay refused to allow Battery "E"'s convoy to cross unless the fare was paid on every vehicle. He may or may not have been legally correct, but the battery was due at a maneuver on the Catawba Peninsula and had to pass through. And the Ohio National Guard headquarters in Columbus said "no" to paying the fare. Two big sergeants dismounted and started walking towards the toll gate, each with a wrench in hand, when the gatekeeper prudently swung the barrier aside.

In 1939, Battery "E" went to Wisconsin in the summer for a live firing practice. On the first night in the field, the men nearly froze; their overcoats were safely locked in the armory across from Battery Park. Louise got a telephone call from "somewhere in Wisconsin." She took young Russ, now four, in her car to the armory; soon a Sandusky police officer showed up in a cruiser. He took a crowbar, broke the lock, and, together, he and Louise loaded the heavy woolen overcoats into their two cars. They drove to the New York Central Railroad Station, placed the coats on a Railway Express car, and, eighteen hours later, the men of Battery "E" had warm overcoats.

In 1939, the battery was sailing from the foot of Columbus Avenue to fire a salute at the 4th of July ceremonies which the Governor was conducting at Put-in-Bay, the site made famous in the War of 1812. Russell forgot his sunglasses, the "Chippewa's" crew was pulling up the gangplank, and Louise decided to give the matter her best. Stuffing Floss and Russ quickly into the car, which she normally drove with Gothic slowness and precision, she careened southward on Columbus Avenue to the family house. Retrieving the offending sunglasses in their leather case from the hall table, she raced northward, screeching to a stop on the dock as the steamer was churning up ugly looking black harbor water. Drawing back her arm, she completed a long forward pass with the leather case, accompanied by resounding cheers from the Guardsmen hanging over the rail.

The following Thanksgiving, 1939, Battery "E" went to Camp Perry, on the lake shore west of Sandusky, for rifle and pistol firing exercises. Louise brought the children over in the family Studebaker, driving carefully through the rows of eight--man wall tents that comprised the encampment. Russell stood in a pile of smoldering ashes on the site where his tent had recently been, only a few boot soles and metal rifle parts visible in the debris.

"Someone put too much fuel in the stove," he said ruefully. "All my stuff is burned up."

In January of 1940, Russell took his young family on their greatest adventure to date. The four of them drove all the way to Miami, Florida, which seemed like a far away tropical wonderland to Ohio people of that era. The trip took five days each way, and roadside accommodations for a family with young children were precarious and far apart. Russ upchucked on Floss's navy blue overcoat, known as the "birdy" coat for the naval petty officer's insignia on the sleeve, as the Studebaker lurched over icy Kentucky roads. Russell stopped the car, assembled the fouled clothes, and started down an embankment for a nearby stream. Moments later, he sank into the deep mud, thigh high, and was saying some words unknown to the children's vocabulary.

In Florida, there was the thrill of white sandy beaches, fresh squeezed orange juice, softly waving palm trees, pink flamingos at the racetrack- all of it indescribable to northern Ohioans accustomed to brief summers on Lake Erie's wave pounded beaches. They saw a Pan American Airways flying boat roar out across the water and disappear into the sunset, bound for England. They purchased two parakeets, one of whom escaped in the hotel lobby and another in the car during the trek home to Sandusky. The memories of this trip would bind them during the coming turmoil that no one could have predicted.

In October, 1940, the 37th Infantry Division of the Ohio National Guard was federalized "for six months, a precaution until Hitler can be brought under control." Captain Ramsey led his battery overland all the way to Hattiesburg, Mississippi, where Camp Shelby was being rushed into completion as a division sized mobilization center. Just getting all the equipment across the eastern United States was actually good training for what was to come.

In February, 1941, Russell called Louise and told her that he had rented a house in Hattiesburg at 621 Walnut Street, right next door to the Municipal Judge. She loaded up Floss and Russ for the long train trek southward. The first night, she sent Russ into the bathroom of the Pullman car to put on his pajamas and brush his teeth. He ran back into the aisle of the car much faster than he had entered the bathroom.

"Mom!" he shouted for all to hear. "Those nuns are in here. They've got all their clothes off!"

Louise had just begun her five year ordeal of managing the family while Russell did what the citizen soldier, however dedicated, shudders to consider: fight an overseas war. An Army Judge Advocate General's Corps colonel called Russell from the Pentagon, shortly after his arrival at Camp Shelby. Would he like to be jump-promoted from captain to lieutenant colonel, transferred to the J.A.G. Corps, and serve out the war as an Army lawyer in the Pentagon? Promotion to full colonel was a sure thing. Would that not be better than serving as a lowly captain of Artillery in a combat unit?

But the colonel did not understand what Russell's commitment to national defense, through the militia, really meant. After all, he could practice law and stay home; he was well beyond draft age and did not have to serve at all. But Nazi evil could only be defeated, he reasoned, by citizen soldiers- America's best- fighting Hitler's legions on the ground, and beating them decisively.

The World War II Years

When Louise and the children arrived in Hattiesburg to take up residence, Russell was already being noticed by officers in higher authority. He had, in fact, already surrendered command of his beloved Battery "E" and joined the Division Staff, as an Assistant G-3, most unusual for a captain.

For eighteen months, Louise and the children learned about life in small town Mississippi, where the grinding poverty of the Great Depression was still everywhere visible, where the southern drawl led to hilarious misunderstandings for Ohioans, and where Black people were required to behave with a servility the Ramseys had never seen. Yet the people of Hattiesburg went far out of their way to extend the most gracious hospitality to these "Yankees" who were, they discovered, wartime small town folk like them, but far from home. Floss would have her first date in Hattiesburg, and Russ would play with the daughter of the Municipal Judge next door. But for Russell, the Hattiesburg months really meant the discovery, at Camp Shelby, that he was a superbly talented soldier, cut out for the exercise of high command.

Russell helped activate a new unit, called a Tank Destroyer Battalion. He wrote reams of organizational detail as the 37th Division abandoned its World War I "square" organization and became a "triangular" division, built upon three infantry regiments with supporting weapons and services. He attracted the notice of Major General Robert S. Beightler, an Ohio public administrator who commanded the 37th Infantry Division throughout the war. Where many National Guard division commanders proved to be incompetent in World War II, Beightler was easily the peer of the Regular Army's finest- a professional soldier who quickly culled out and sent home the politically appointed officers who could not adapt to leadership in modern warfare. He demanded the best from his men, fought for them in all situations, and received the greatest loyalty and devotion from them. He was arguably the top National Guard officer of World War II.

Captain Ramsey was sent to the Artillery School at Fort Sill to take the Battery Officers Course. Here he found that his artillery knowledge was strong, but that the U.S. Army was still teaching World War I tactics in an era when Hitler's forces were rewriting the books on fire and maneuver tactics. Somehow, he learned how to adapt without criticizing and making enemies, the fine art of succeeding without antagonizing. And General Beightler quietly noted that his lawyer-captain, prematurely gray at the temples, was a born wartime leader of troops.

On the famous Louisiana Maneuver of 1941, the largest array of military forces ever to maneuver on U.S. terrain in peacetime, Russell deepened his military knowledge. He wrote a tactical plan which, when executed by the 37th Division's maturing combat elements, resulted in the capture, verified by a field umpire, of a budding Regular Army officer, Brig. Gen. George Patton, Jr. Patton fumed and cursed over the umpire's decision to let his entire command group be bagged by, of all things, a National Guard unit.

Russell's sister Jean, now a graduate student in geology at the University of Chicago, made the long trek to Hattiesburg to visit during their Christmas in Mississippi. So did Helen and Ted Harten, as well as Fred and Helen Zuck, old Sandusky friends and business associates.

In mid 1942, the 37th Division received orders to stage out of Indian Town Gap, Pennsylvania, thence to England for the Allied invasion of Northern Africa. All 18,500 men and their equipment went to this quaint Pennsylvania Dutch district on long trains; Russell wrote the movement orders. Louise drove the family overland, home to Sandusky. The family house had been rented out when Russell and Louise figured out that Hitler was not going to give up in six months, and she rented a two-bedroom apartment on the third floor of the Eureka Apartment, just two blocks south of the family house on Columbus Avenue. Briefly, however, the family stayed with her parents, Merritt and Janet Wilcox ("Oh-oh and Pop"), some six blocks farther south on Columbus Avenue.

The 37th Division was to stage a review for Governor John Bricker of Ohio at Indiantown Gap, then ship out to Europe. Louise drove the children on the Pennsylvania Turnpike, a thrilling new experience in those days, to Annville, Pennsylvania, and rented an apartment in an old stone farmhouse from an Amish family. For several days, Russell would pop in on short notice to spend a few hours with the children. Then, suddenly, the Division's orders were changed. They would go to the Pacific Theater via San Francisco, and right away. Russell wrote the movement order for the trek westward, on very short notice, and Louise took the children to live in Sandusky.

Russell was promoted to major enroute to the Pacific, and the 37th Division was placed in the Fiji Islands for extensive training in jungle warfare. Then, the division was assigned to Lieutenant General Oscar W. Griswold's legendary XIVth Corps, the ground component of the Navy's Central Pacific Command. A few months after arriving in the Fiji Islands, the 37th Division was tapped for the invasion of the Solomon Islands, slugging their way first into New Georgia and then fighting an extended campaign in Bougainville. The operation was rough, casualties were heavy, and the 37th Division did not get the publicity accorded to the Marine Corps units which were part of XIVth Corps. Russell later would chide another Sanduskyan, his wife's cousin, Marine Corps Brigadier General Robert L. Denig, wartime Chief of Marine Corps Publicity, for "making the world think that the Marines did all the fighting in the Solomons."

Russell was promoted to lieutenant colonel and recommended for the Legion of Merit, a new medal that was supposed to be for officers who acted heroically in battle but under conditions of great responsibility. The medal came through, and he was honored again by being named battalion commander of the 3d Battalion, 145th Infantry, a rare thing for an artillery officer. His battalion endured the furies of Hell in weeks of bloody, foxhole-to-foxhole jungle combat with the Japanese Imperial Army. When things calmed down he was returned to the Division Staff as G-3, Operations Officer. An Army Commendation Medal and the Combat Infantry Badge were added to his decorations. Later, when the Legion of Merit became a more or less routine award for senior officers in both peacetime and in battle, he discovered that General Beightler would have preferred to have awarded him the Distinguished Service Medal or the Silver Star instead of the Legion of Merit. Perhaps as a signal, Russell's Army Commendation Medal was revoked and upgraded to the more prestigious Bronze Star.

Russell enjoyed a few days of Rest and Relaxation tour ("R & R") in New Zealand, staying with a delightful family in Aukland who had, like so many Kiwis and Aussies, already lost a son with the British Empire forces fighting the Germans in North Africa. Returned to battle for the last of the Solomon Islands Campaign, he learned that the 37th Division would be part of the shock troops that would spearhead the recapture of the Philippines, and that General Douglas MacArthur would exercise overall command of this campaign. Then, he learned with great joy that he had been selected to return to the United States, for a total of about ten weeks, to attend the U.S. Army Command & General Staff College at Ft. Leavenworth, Kansas.

Russell and Louise rented the upstairs of an old house in a poor neighborhood in the town of Leavenworth, that early spring of 1944. Floss attended a public high school and discovered that her classmates thought her explanation, "My Daddy's at Leavenworth" meant that he was an inmate in the Federal Prison which coexists there with Army activities. Russ attended the Army dependent school at Ft. Leavenworth, finding out quickly that the Regular Army children did not welcome the sons and daughters of wartime officers. Russell found out why.

As late as March, 1944, the U.S. Army still held a cadre of Regular Army officers, mostly West Point graduates, at Ft. Leavenworth, to teach battle doctrine to the huge, expanding wartime force. These officers had not been overseas; many were captains or junior majors and had never seen combat. For them, the Army was their career and their life. For Russell and the temporary, wartime officers who were the students at the Command & General Staff College, the Army was a temporary vehicle with which to defeat the Germans and the Japanese forces. Most were majors or lieutenant colonels; all wore combat medals, recently earned in battle. Coming to Ft. Leavenworth was, to them, a way to get some time at home in the United States, with their families. Listening to a Regular Army captain expound upon inflexible World War I tactical concepts that did not work in modern warfare was a low priority.

As graduation approached for Russell, he faced return to the Pacific Theater, so one day he obtained permission to take young Russ to class with him. Some 1,200 officers sat at little wooden tables in a huge Qounset hut; electric fans moved desultory Kansas summer air and impertinent flies around overhead. A handsome captain with two service ribbons, no combat awards, droned on and on, using a public address system that crackled annoyingly.

"And so," he queried, "what is the correct ratio of combat forces that a battalion, regiment, or division may expend in the defense of the water supply source?" (Russell's lesson outline showed that the correct school answer was eight percent.) The captain ran his finger down a student roster, then said, "Lt. Col. Ramsey, will you answer this question please?"

Russell walked down the aisle to the stage, picked up the microphone, and answered the question. "In the situation we were given," he said, "the platoon defending the regimental water point would be adequate until the enemy changed his actions and attacked the water point with a larger force. Then, the defense would have to be strengthened."

"But Col. Ramsey," persisted the captain, "what is the correct ratio of troops? Does your solution meet those guidelines or not?"

"Captain," said Russell, as interest picked up in the sweaty auditorium, "when a battalion, regiment, or division finds its waterpoint threatened, it must defend that source with whatever it takes." Noticing the disapproving expression on the captain's face, he reiterated his point. "My battalion on Bougainville had the 37th Division's water source within our lines. The Japs threw a reinforced battalion attack at us, and several follow-up attacks. I had thirty-eight men killed in the defense. You do what it takes. A division cannot fight without water."

There was a moment of dead silence, and then the students broke into loud cheers. Russell was never a confrontational person, but the situation had brought out the courtroom tactician in him, had challenged his very loyalty to the citizen soldiers with whom he was making his stand in the Pacific. He sat down quietly and began reading the next tactical situation in his student handout material.

For Louise, the Leavenworth interlude included calling the local police several times when the next door neighbor's son would go into violent rages and attack his mother with a shovel or an ax. But all too soon it ended, and her beloved Russell, on a hot summer day in 1944, boarded a train for San Francisco, thence to the Solomon Islands to rejoin the 37th Division. Louise, Floss, and Russ went home to the family house at 1311, giving up the apartment, and their daily routine once again peaked with the arrival of the postman and the possibility of a "V-Mail" envelope from the Pacific Theater.

Russell's Leavenworth training coupled now with his staff and combat command experience to render him invaluable in the forthcoming invasion of the Philippines, which, the experts believed, would culminate in 1945 and pave the way for the assault on the Japanese homeland in 1946. Russell, appointed G-3 (Operations Officer), prepared the 37th Division loading plan to get the 18,500 men and all their equipment to the Lingayan Gulf in the correct sequence for disembarkation onto landing craft in what would be the Pacific Theater's largest amphibious assault, second in size only to the Normandy Invasion, in World War II and world military history. Someone in the G-3 Section at the next higher echelon, Lt. Gen. Oscar W. Griswold's legendary XIVth Corps, noticed that the overall Corps loading plan did not meet with U.S. Navy approval, save for the 37th Division's portion. Russell was loaned to XIVth Corps for a month to orchestrate the Corps loading and movement plan. Once, he had to defend the overall Army plan at a tense meeting aboard the Navy flagship while General Douglas MacArthur and other top Army brass scowled at three- and four-star Navy admirals. When the meeting ended, Russell exited the buzzing command center and vomited in the passageway outside, unsure of whether the petty service partisanship shown by these much ballyhooed senior commanders was the true cause of his upset stomach. After all, he was a militia lieutenant colonel who did not even have to be serving in uniform, much less in the Pacific, and he had been forced to referee, as it were, the loading of Army troops on Navy ships among the top professional military brasshats in the Pacific Theater.

On January 9, 1945, Russell led the 37th Division's forward command post element ashore at Lingayen Gulf, on the west coast of Luzon. The landing met only light opposition on the beach, but XIVth Corps, in general, and the 37th Division, in particular, soon ran into the heaviest combined arms fighting in the Pacific Theater. Where the recapture of Leyte, the previous October, had required the defeat of light, reinforced infantry backed by inadequate reserves, the Luzon Campaign became the only segment of World War II in the Pacific that was fought on a scale equal to the recapture of France and the low countries, and the conquering of Nazi Germany. Especially galling to the men of the 37th Division was the fact of General MacArthur's personal involvement in recapturing the Philippines on terms that would justify his own historical perceptions of his role, and in his assignment of the "glory roles" to the 1st Cavalry Division and the llth Airborne Division, both commanded by Regular Army major generals with whom he shared a military career.

On February 3, 1945, the 37th Division battered its way into Manilla, having overcome much heavier resistance than the divisions on its flanks, only to learn that the newspapers back home were screaming, "1st Cavalry Troopers Race into Manila; MacArthur Declares City Retaken." The 37th then earned, with Regular Army Major General Oscar W. Griswold's full support and later recognition, the XIVth Corps' task of clearing thousands of suicidally inclined Japanese defenders out of the Intramuros, the old Spanish walled city of 18th century construction. Russell wrote and coordinated the daylight assault in small boats across the Pasig River, and the breaching and retaking of the Intramuros. Thousands of civilian internees, mostly Filipinos but some Europeans and Americans, were saved in the process. In February, 1966, Russell returned to Manila with young Russ, then a captain commanding a company in the 1st Air Cavalry Division in Vietnam. Young Russ was on five days' "R & R," and Russell delighted in showing his soldier son the battlefield that had been in Manila, 22 years before. As they stood by the Pasig River, contemplating the audacious amphibious assault that the 37th's men had done there, a Filipino man came up, read the name tag on young Russ's Army uniform, turned to Russell, and said, "You must be Col. Ramsey who led the American troops here. They saved many of us." Russell was pleased but not particularly surprised at this Filipino who remembered for so long; thus deep has been the blood bond between Americans and Filipinos.

The 37th took high but necessary casualties during the liberation of Manila, rejecting, on Russell's decision, the proffered help of an untried Ranger Battalion which planned to scale the walls of the Intramuros on ropes, Hollywood style. At the Manila Hotel, where General MacArthur had once resided in prewar splendor as Field Marshall of the Philippine Constabulary, Russell found 37th Division G.I.s restraining would-be sweeping details from MacArthur's Headquarters; they had been told to clean up the Boss's old residence while dozens of Japanese soldiers still fought from inside.

In early March, resistance ceased in Manila; 16,665 Japanese soldiers and sailors lay dead within the Intramuros, alone. The 37th Division was now pointed northward for the clearance of northern Luzon, where at least 75,000 Japanese troops still held out in well prepared positions. Russell's promotion to colonel came through, and he was given a second award of the Bronze Star with "V" (for valor). The old mountain city of Baguio fell to the U.S. VIth Army, and the 37th Division ran into some of the toughest fighting in all of World War II in the Cagayan Valley, which had to be cleared prior to the final race northward to Tarlac on the northern coast of Luzon.

In April, defending Japanese forces made a stand at the bridge over the Irisan River. Several 37th Division units and forces from other divisions were converging in the region's restrictive mountainous terrain, and the Japanese were using caves to conceal mortars and light artillery pieces to interdict road junctions and narrow spots on the primitive roads. Newly appointed to the post of Chief of Staff, Russell operated the division's forward command post. At one point, forward motion - utterly vital to any attacking force- ceased; ominously, wrecked U.S. vehicles plus wounded and dead U.S. troops were bottlenecked on the torturous roadnet. Russell took personal control of the situation to coordinate artillery, aircraft, and ground advance of the various units.

For several hours, Russell ran about the battle area directing counterfire and troop movement; Japanese mortar and artillery rounds were exploding continuously all around. Occasionally a stream of bullets from a Nimbu machine gun went zipping and whining by. Russell got the attacking force moving again to force the passage of the key bridge across the Irisan. Crouching with his forward control group in a cemetery, he was suddenly aware that a Japanese mortarman had their range from a hidden site. He ordered the group to disperse and take cover. Just as he and the last two men were preparing to make their own sprint for safety, a mortar round exploded some twelve feet away, sending a dozen coin-sized jagged metal fragments into Russell's left arm and leg. The others, too, were hit, and he had to stanch his own bleeding, then wait out the silencing of the unseen mortar gunner by artillery counterfire before being carried off by litter to the division forward aid station.

For this action, Russell was awarded the Silver Star and the Purple Heart. He used his recuperation days to dictate and edit a report of the battle, returning to duty with left arm and leg still heavily bandaged and full of stitches.

Half way around the world, it was a cold, drizzly April day in northern Ohio. Floss walked briskly home for lunch from Sandusky High School, where she was a 9th grader, and Russ popped in from his 3d grade class at nearby Campbell Elementary School. Louise was seated in the library with Arthur J. "Buddy" Little, a World War I veteran who, with wife Lucille, was a favorite bridge and bowling companion of Russell and Louise in happier times. Louise held a telegram from the War Department:

"Wounded in action against the enemy in the Asia-Pacific Theater...", the impersonal words which tried to pretend that the reader did now know where the battle had occurred, for military security reasons. Louise sat quietly in her chair, occasionally wiping her eyes; Floss and Russ, once assured by the kindly Bud Little that their father would survive, simply tried to imagine him in bandages and, no doubt, in great pain. They returned teary-eyed to their schools for the afternoon session, wondering silently if they would ever again see their father. People were kind but unsure of what to say, and, in that era, there was no television program with "instant experts" telling the nation about how to deal with wartime trauma. The window flags all over Sandusky had red borders, white fields, and blue stars for living servicemen, gold stars for those who had already paid the final price; these were far stronger testimony to the sacrifices of a nation at war than the televised hoop-la attending the Persian Gulf Conflict that coincided with the final hours of Russell's life.

As the 37th Division drove ever northward, the world political situation changed radically, forcing changes on the battlefield and at home. In May of 1945, Nazi Germany surrendered to the Allied Forces in Europe; since many more U.S. troops were serving in this, the primary theater of the war, the "V.E. Day" (Victory in Europe) celebrations turned towns and cities all over America upside down with delirious excitement. Floss and Russ heard schoolmates tell how their brothers and fathers were coming home soon. And while, in actuality, demobilization was not that rapid and thousands of troops were being redeployed to the Asian-Pacific Theater for the assault on the Japanese homeland, word reached 37th Division troops in northern Luzon that "other guys" were getting demobilized before the fight was really over. The impact on morale was staggering. Only a combat veteran who has experienced war with the perceived lack of full national support can comprehend what Russell now faced as he directed units of the 37th Division to advance on Japanese caves and tunnels, occupied by men whose only goal was to die in place for the Emperor, and whose only route to heroism lay in "taking some Americans along." American soldiers, imbued with a sense of purpose in life, could grasp the fight against Tojoism, Fascism, and Nazism; but giving one's life as, perhaps, the last casualty in a war that might soon end, against men who actually wanted to die... that was a different thing. The bravery with which the men of the 37th Division faced this new challenge was due, in part, to officers from top to bottom who placed themselves at the forefront of the action.

Thus it was in early August that Russell raced to the head of a convoy which was stalled on a precipitous mountain road, the lead element of the division advance. Here, a T-24 light tank had been hit by a lucky Japanese artillery round, and was now lying astride the road and blocking further advance. As the lead unit prepared to push the disabled vehicle off the road, Russell spread a map across the hood of his jeep. Several officers bent their heads downward to follow his plan for renewing the advance. Suddenly a platoon of Japanese infantrymen emerged from a cave; their initial fire dropped several U.S. soldiers, and the platoon leader charged toward Russell with Samurai sword raised high, his pistol cracking in the other hand. One bullet zipped past Russell's ear as he drew his .45 caliber semi-automatic pistol, fired once, and dropped the Japanese lieutenant no more than ten feet away. And when the Japanese surrender offer was announced on August 10th, the men of the 37th Division still took casualties for two more weeks as Japanese troops, out of touch with their chain of command or unwilling to accept defeat, fought on to their own deaths. Yet in Sandusky, on the night of "V.J. Day", Floss and Russ watched people dancing in the street on Columbus Avenue in front of their house, and the next day well meaning people told them, "Hey, your father's coming home, isn't that great!"

In fact, there was heavy December snow on the ground all across Ohio when Russell came home. His final three months in Luzon were tumultuous. Lt. Gen. Okamato, commanding the 10th Japanese Infantry Division, surrendered to Russell on August 16th, presenting him with a priceless Samurai sword forged in February of 1550. Russell oversaw the outloading of the entire division through the Subic Bay Navy Base, and, en route home, detoured to Texas, there to share his sympathy with the parents of "Tex," his jeep driver who was killed during a Japanese ambush in the war's final weeks. Louise left Floss and Russ at home for a few days with the family of Wesley Hartung, the beloved Choirmaster at Grace Episcopal Church, while she went west on crowded wartime transportation for a joyous reunion with her husband. Russell's stepmother Helen and her husband Ted then brought Floss and Russ down to Columbus, a six hour drive in heavy snow, to see their father. They had to endure a testimonial dinner by Columbus big-wigs before they could snuggle in the back seat with him, still wearing his Army blouse with gleaming colonel's eagles and three rows of combat awards.

This time it was really over. Louise, Floss, and Russ could now hear with incredulity about such things as "Operation OLYMPIC," the planned invasion of Japan in January, 1946 that would have found the 37th Division declared "too damaged for further battle action" by February, following the attack on the homeland. Russell shared quietly with a few people his belief that he, personally, would not have survived this assault. Maj. Gen. Robert S. Beightler, the 37th's magnificent wartime commander, was recognized with the award of a Regular Army major general's commission, a stupendous honor at a time when career senior officers were being reduced by two ranks in order to stay on active duty, and mothers paraded before the White House demanding that President Harry S. Truman "bring home the boys" or risk impeachment.

Russell and Louise decided that a family trip was necessary. Floss and Russ were given six weeks of school assignments, and, in January and February of 1946, the family rented a gray shingled cottage called "Mandalay" on the beach at Naples, Florida, just north of the famous "Mile Long Pier." During their joyful sojourn they visited often with "Hellie and Ted," whose winter home was about thirty miles north at Ft. Myers. They listened in awe as Russell recounted gently the flavor of that final, furious combat with the Japanese Empire. The owner of "Mandalay" cottage let it be known that he would sell the property for about $10,000, but Russell could not scrape up that kind of cash and was distrustful of Naples real estate ventures when the late 1920s "bust" there was still visible in 1946. The property, in the 1980s, could have been sold to condominium developers for several million dollars! Yet the "Mandalay" excursion would always be the family's romantic moment in time. Russell, Louise, and the children dreamed unrealistically of fun unending- trips, singing together, games, jokes- that would surely come, now that war was no more. They could hardly have been more wrong in their estimate of the future.

1946 - 1960; the Attorney and the General

In the summer of 1946, Russell brought his family to Columbus, Ohio where Maj. Gen. Robert S. Beightler was Commander, Ohio Military District, at historic Fort Hayes. Claire Beightler treated Louise like a sister and indulged the children as if they were part of her own close and loving family. Russell had just set up a new law partnership in Sandusky with the distinguished William E. Didelius, a former F.B.I. agent and concert organist. Louise had taken great pride in decorating the office with framed prints of wartime sketches done in the Philippines by the combat artist E. J. Gollriehs. Russell steadfastly refused to display symbols of battlefield violence, such as Lt. Gen. Okamato's sword, in his office. But in June, 1946 he was refused even a colonel's commission in the peacetime 37th Division, as the Ohio politicians who did not fight the war now reasserted political control in the convenient absence of the previous commander, Gen. Beightler, who always insisted on military standards over political favoritism.

So it came as a bolt out of the sky when Gen. Beightler, speaking now, of course, for the Regular Army, made known to Russell his offer. In the rank of colonel, U.S. Army Reserve, Russell was to activate the 83d Infantry Division, which had fought proudly as a mobilization force in Europe during the war. The Army Reserve was to have several such divisions, and the idea in forming them was to counter-balance the National Guard, over which the War Department had less control in peacetime. Command of a division, of course, called for a two-star officer, but Gen. Beightler could make no future promises, for he was being re-assigned to Washington D.C.

On a bleak evening in the summer of 1946, Russell assumed command of a few dozen World War II veterans at a quiet ceremony inside the World War II bomber plant that stood idle and empty beside the Cleveland Airport. The newspapers, even in Sandusky, covered the affair as little more than a brief announcement. Interest picked up in Sandusky, however, when it was announced that "Russell A. Ramsey, local attorney and a combat veteran of the Pacific Theater, was being promoted to brigadier general, U.S. Army Reserve, in which rank he would command a regional force to be headquartered in Cleveland." One might expect that promotion to flag rank, in a small town, would bring legal clients back to an attorney who had been gone for 4 1/2 years to fight the war. And indeed, in short order Russell was again representing such fine Sandusky companies as the Wagner Quarries, the Esmond Dairy, and the Western Security Bank; but he also learned that some of his clients had been taken for good by an attorney firm in the same office building, men who declined to serve in wartime. Not once in Russell's lifetime did he ever express disapproval of these men, nor of their actions.

As the 83d Division began to expand to full size, Russell brought to bear two traits that would make it second to none as a citizen-soldier division that stood always ready for mobilization. He applied Gen. Beightler's no-excuses philosophy about military professionalism. What men could not learn in battle, they could at least study at a service school on short tours of active duty. For commanders who conducted unit training that was desultory or unrealistic he had no mercy. But Russell had a second leadership resource that Gen. Beightler, himself, did not possess. As a lawyer, with a history of fighting some battles for legal justice, Russell could use his position as a prominent corporate attorney to help his Army Reserve soldiers when they were caught in the cracks between military duty and civilian employment. Thus, when Eastern Airlines used sly tactics to pass over an employee for promotion because he had reported to Army Reserve duty at a time not desired by the company, the airline found itself facing a wide array of legal actions which Russell initiated as Chairman of the Ethics Committee of the Ohio Bar Association. Eastern Airlines prudently and quickly reversed its decision. One of Russell's soldiers was taken to the cleaners by scam artists whose frozen food and home freezer plan resulted in years of huge, legally enforceable bills but little meat. This company suddenly found itself facing criminal charges in several cities at once, where lawyers who were also Reservists just happened to live, and also knew how to fight back from within the law. The scam artists were put out of business, and Ohio consumer law was made more just as a consequence.

But in civilian life, Russell followed in the footsteps of his father during the post-war years. His war record, military rank, legal standing, organizational skill, and fund raising abilities combined to earn him appointments to leadership boards throughout the district. Thus, he spent several years each as Senior Warden of Grace Episcopal Church, as Vice President of the Board of the Western Security Bank, and as President of Good Samaritan Hospital; each of these institutions underwent huge expansion and modernization programs during Russell's tenure. The law firm of "Ramsey and Didelius" was a fixture in the northern Ohio legal landscape for thirty years. Bill Didelius matched Russell's commitment to public service by serving a stint as the tough, reformist Prosecutor of Erie County, putting some long overdue crooks into prison at personal risk; and by his unflagging support of the musical program at Grace Episcopal Church. Indeed, it was Bill Didelius' recognition of the musical value in Grace Church's four manual tracker (mechanically activated pipes) organ which caused Russell to lead the drive for expensive rehabilitation work in lieu of modernization with an electric organ of lesser artistic merit. The result was that RCA cut records by famous organists on the priceless instrument. Coupled with Wesley Hartung's Grace Church Choristers, the sacred music program achieved fame.

While Russell became a figure in demand for occasional speeches on defense, law, and citizenship, he avoided the well known proclivity of some war veterans to recount, with growing exaggeration, the ugly details of battle. Instead, he read profoundly on such issues as the United Nations, the rising world alignment called the "Cold War" from 1947 through 1989, and the duties of citizenship in such issues as the continuing military draft. And in an age when applied psychology was not part of daily life and family process, Russell made essentially a spiritual adjustment to the horrors of war he had experienced. The rector of Grace Episcopal Church invited a Japanese clergyman to visit Sandusky, to participate in church services, and to administer Holy Communion at the altar. Choir boys and their families as well sucked in their breath when General Ramsey, who was known to be the community's hero in the war against Japan, marched erectly up the aisle between the choir stalls, and knelt devoutly to receive the Sacrament. If the Japanese clergyman knew the identity of the gray haired man to whose lips he pressed the silver chalice, he did not show it. In the car, on the way home, Louise observed that the visiting clergyman seemed to know the service well.

"Indeed he does," said Russell. "There are many good people among the Japanese."

As Russell ascended in military rank, community leadership, and legal standing, so, too, were his children growing up. He never lamented the 4 1/2 missed years but seemed to want to enter in at the present level. The observance of family dinner in the dining room, with meaningful conversation, was a ritual demanded by both Russell and Louise. Floss had some stimulating teachers at Sandusky High School, and she now enjoyed lively intellectual conversations with her father at these family dinners. Once, Russell quoted some bit of erudition from his own college days at Princeton University, following which Floss located his old textbook and discovered that the edges of the pages on that topic had never been cut so that one could read them. Russell personally took Floss to Cleveland to take the College Boards Exam (Standard Achievement Test- SAT), and, on the way home they impulsively bought a German shepherd dog whose tenure in the family home lasted less than two years, due to his loud, nervous barking. Russell took an active role in the college selection process with Floss, and he was delighted when she chose Wellesley. He once spent a three day father-daughter session with her at the campus.

Russell took young Russ hunting in a rented marsh near Cedar Point during the 1947 duck season. Russ insisted on taking along the sweet but unruly German Shepherd, named Arno, even though Russell stated repeatedly that "police dogs don't hunt ducks." Russ had learned, by this time, his father's story about the time when Russell K. fell over the protruding gasline fixture on the front lawn during a kite flying effort, long ago. Now it was young Russ's turn to be overcome with laughter when his own father, Russell A., plunged six feet downward into the duck blind as he tried to lower the squirming dog Arno.

But storm clouds also beset Russell and his family during this period, clouds that cast shadows which never lifted at all. Prone to executive overwork in a big way, in an era when the medical profession did not recognize the aerobic fitness needs of people who do office work, Russell suffered a mild heart attack in the spring of 1950. While the valve damage apparently was minimal, it showed Louise that her husband was mortal, and that his career and achievements which she treasured with all her heart could threaten Russell's health. The Army Reserve took the matter seriously enough to delay Russell's promotion to major general (two stars) for several months until heart specialists could certify that his condition was not debilitating.

In 1948, Russell bought the family a 20 foot motor boat, an open runabout of fine mahogany with the lap strake hull construction done by Bill Lyman, a legendary Sandusky boat builder. Floss and Russ loved the outings with their father and friends on this boat, named "Bulavanaka," the Fijian word Russell had learned for "a very tremendous, fine 'Hello to you'." But once they were caught in a dangerous storm, right in Sandusky Bay, and only the seaworthiness built into Lyman boats, and Russell's boating skill, saved them from swamping and possible drowning.

Thereafter, Louise would never again go out in the boat, and Russell sold it in 1952.

In the summer of 1950, the Korean Conflict broke out; Army National Guard units performed badly, at first, and the 83d Reserve Division was notified that it would be the next citizen unit activated if another full division were required. For the next two years, the 83d "Thunderbolt" Division's name sat before force planners in the Pentagon, but it was never called. Nevertheless, this issue, plus Russell's predisposition to overwork now began to take an emotional toll upon Louise, and her emotional distress manifested itself in a series of vexing health problems and family conflicts that never fully left her until her death in 1990.

In June, 1951, Floss graduated from Wellesley with a B.A. in French literature and political science. She had taken her junior year at the Institute de Sciences Politiques, in Paris, and was a gifted linguist at a time when French was still the world's primary diplomatic language. But she had been dating John H. Waldock for several years, and she wanted to be married. Jack Waldock was the second son of Bill and Ernestine Waldock, whose family home on Wayne Street was just two blocks from the Ramsey house on Columbus Avenue. Bill Waldock co-owned the Waldock Packing Co. with his brother Fred. Young Jack had graduated from Ohio State University's animal husbandry program in just three years, earning the highest grades ever registered en route, and winning national championships in competitive meat judging. With his brother, Bill, he was a world class trap shooter, owning many titles, and in the early 1950s he established himself as the outstanding amateur golfer in the district. In 1951 he was employed at his father's meat packing plant on Perkins Avenue, the start of a career that would take him eventually to become a pioneer in commodities trading.

So on September 8, 1951, Russell escorted his daughter on his arm at the wedding in Grace Episcopal Church, site of his own marriage to Louise 29 years before. The young couple resided briefly at the Erie Apartment on Columbus Avenue following their wedding trip, then bought a charming brick house on Scott Street where they lived until 1958. During the 1950s, Floss and Jack presented Russell with three granddaughters whom he adored: Becky, in 1952; Beth, in 1954; and Laurie, in 1957. Perhaps remembering the great trek out west with his father just after his mother had died, long ago, he made it a policy to take one big trip with each of his grandchildren. Another big event in Russell's life during the 1950s was the decision to sell the family home on Columbus Avenue. In 1954, Russell and Louise moved to 413 Columbus Avenue, a quaint old stone house listed in the *Sandusky Register* of *Historic Homes*. From this location Russell could walk to his office on East Washington Row, and to the nearby Erie County Court house.

Russell was a wise enough father to see that his son Russ revered his father's career, but wanted to choose his own path. He discussed such options as attending Princeton University and Ohio State Law School with his son, but Russ had been smitten with the bug to attend the U.S. Military Academy at West Point after meeting several of its graduates. Appointments to West Point still started, in those days, with the favorable nod from a Congressman, and Sandusky's Congressman Alvin Weichel made it clear to Russell and to his son that the favorable nod would be given, always, to a football player, since this practice, he stated, resulted in the sensible outcome of courtesy tickets to the Army-Navy Game which the good Congressman could then bestow upon his friends. Young Russ did his homework on the system and discovered that one could enter West Point competitively, without benefit of political favoritism, by attending a military school that carried the U.S. Army rating of an "Honor School, and then by winning a place in the top ten from among the 300 or so annual competitive applicants in this category.

By disdaining to throw his military rank and political standing as a Republic party member at the situation, Russell thus earned for his son the dignity of winning his own way to his goal. Russell took Russ to look over Howe Military School in Indiana, his own alma mater; but Russ was a competitive swimmer, hopeful of regional or higher honors in the sport, and

Howe had neither pool nor swim team. The beautiful old Staunton Military Academy in Virginia offered not only a championship swim team but also a stupendous track record of grooming boys for the service academies. So Russell supported his son totally and from the heart in his wish to attend Staunton, even though the financial burden must have been heavy, and he surely would have liked for young Russ to attend Howe.

In 1953, Russell attended Russ's graduation from Staunton in his general's uniform. His heart must nearly have burst with pride, for young Russ in two years at Staunton had been captain of the state championship swim team; editor of the school newspaper; and had garnered competitive Honor School appointments to West Point, Annapolis, the Coast Guard Academy, and to Princeton's Naval ROTC scholarship program. So while Princeton University, with all expenses paid by the Navy, was an option for his son, Russell again declined to pressure Russ to attend his alma mater, instead taking great pride in having a son who was a cadet at West Point. Nevertheless, during a visit to the Academy he pointed out to Russ how he had led the winning charge by the Princeton ROTC polo team against Army in 1924 at the Riding Hall.

Russell was careful to show his son the nuances of the delicate relationships between the Regular Army and the Reserve forces, more by anecdote than by didactic approach. Russell's 83d Reserve Division remained, in the late 1950s, the top rated combat division in the Reserve force structure. Young Russ had attended two weeks of Reserve Summer Training Camp with his father at Camp Breckinridge, Kentucky, in July, 1950, serving as a barracks orderly. Now, during his 30 days' summer leave from West Point in 1956, he requested permission to serve as a Platoon Commander in the 83d Division's Basic Training Company for two weeks. Sadly, Russell became seriously ill and could not attend; his wartime combat friend Brig. Gen. Richard McNelly filled in as Acting Division Commander for the encampment. McNelly, in off-duty moments, taught young Russ many things about his father's World War II service that the family had never known.

In June, 1957, Russell again donned his uniform to watch the Army Chief of Staff, General Maxwell D. Taylor, hand young Russ his diploma and commission as a 2d lieutenant in the Army's infantry branch. On the day before graduation, the Class of 1957 had resurrected a 19th century West Point tradition, breaking ranks at the Graduation Parade to run wildly toward the crowd, and Gen. Taylor had disciplined the violators in great anger, since the event was picked up on national television and embarrassed the Army no small amount. Russell may have been the only Army general present who was taking pictures of his own son in the act of running foolishly across the parade ground, and hoping that the brass hats who ran West Point would not be too harsh in their reaction. And in June, 1957, during Russ's 30 days' summer leave, he served as aide-de-camp for his father during the 83d Division's annual summer training at Camp Breckinridge.

In April, 1958, Russell and Louise returned to Hattiesburg, Mississippi, where they had powerful memories of World War II mobilization days. Russell's sister Jean came over from nearby Jackson, Mississippi with her husband, a medical doctor, and Floss and Jack also made the long trek down from Ohio. The occasion had all the ingredients of a storybook romance. Young Russ was marrying the girl next door, or, in this case the girl who had lived next door to the Ramsey family during their two year sojourn in the rented house in Hattiesburg. He had "re-met" her in 1957, en route to Army training at Ft. Benning, Georgia, using an old address supplied by Louise. She was Linda Stevens, daughter of a retired Hattiesburg Municipal Judge; following the wedding, Russ and Linda took up residence in Army quarters at Ft. Campbell, Kentucky. In January, 1959, their new daughter Ellen became Russell's fourth grandchild; he flew down from Sandusky to take pictures for the family in Sandusky to see.

In 1958, Louise was discovered to have a breast lump, non-malignant; it was the era of the great overkill in American surgery. At the University Hospitals in Cleveland, she underwent a radical double mastectomy, done by physicians as skilled as any in the land. Twenty years later, the procedure would have been considered excessive or even unnecessary; worse yet, the medical profession did not comprehend the need for psychiatric consultation with patients undergoing traumatic surgery. This procedure altered Louise's life horribly, and it meant that Russell would spend the rest of his days worrying about Louise's health problems and their emotional byproducts.

The 1960s are often said to be a tumultuous era in American history, and they certainly were for Russell. In retrospect, one can see that the events of the era to come might easily have embittered him, for many things would challenge the commitments to the law and to national defense that were the cornerstones of his life. It was his intense religious strength, challenged by Japanese mortar shells, honed by difficult family experiences, and developed through painstaking Scriptural study that brought him through the uncertain era with his faith renewed and strengthened. The decade opened for Russell with nothing more unusual than Louise's increasing health troubles, and the intense pressures of his work schedule. His challenges, at the end of the 1950s, were personal, not moral or ideological; but that was soon to change.

1961-1973; Community Leader & General Emeritus

Russell and Louise were always staunch Republicans. The victory of John F. Kennedy in November, 1960 jolted them a bit, and soon they discovered that Russ, now training Latin American military personnel in the former Panama Canal Zone, was a Kennedy fan. The reasons were specific more than ideological; J.F.K., as President, took a personal interest in Latin American security issues that involved the Army, and Russ was teaching anti-guerrilla warfare in Spanish. But then the Kennedy Administration made a little known decision that affected Russell's life profoundly, even though he never would talk about it.

Robert S. McNamara was brought in from the Ford Motor Co. to impose "whiz kid" management techniques on the Pentagon as a reformist U.S. Secretary of Defense. Long on idealism and belief in "scientific management," woefully ignorant of national security and military history, McNamara and J.F.K. announced that they would abolish the Army and Air Force National Guard, leaving all the militia forces under Department of Defense control. When the U.S. National Guard Bureau pulled out all its political stops in opposition, McNamara did a clumsy reversal in order to retain key votes in Congress for the administration. He announced that the "overlapping and inefficient combat divisions in the Army Reserve would be eliminated," making a mockery of his earlier pronouncement that the National Guard's divisions were the ones which were full of administrative deadwood and combat unreadiness. In essence, he abandoned the goal of centralizing control over the state militia, which would have reversed nearly two centuries of U.S. historical practice, and went for the lesser goal of cutting the Reserve Components' budget within the Department of Defense. By doing this, of course, he was cutting out the citizen soldier divisions of the Army Reserve which really were combat ready, and leaving extant several National Guard divisions that later showed their ineptitude. The division of powers between the national government and the states was thereby preserved, but citizen military readiness actually went down.

Throughout the Kennedy-Johnson years, the 83d Reserve Division was steadily cut and gutted; by 1964, when Russell's mandatory retirement age of 60 had been reached, the once-proud Army Reserve divisions were mere training commands with a fraction of their soldiers. Russell's retirement observances conducted by the 83d Division were beautifully dignified testimonies to a commander who was genuinely loved and admired. But Russell's retirement from the Army consisted of a canned little ceremony at Ft. Meade, Maryland, then the regional headquarters over Army Reserve affairs in Ohio. When a major general retires from the Regular Army or from a Reserve Component, the award of the Distinguished Service Medal is virtually automatic, especially if the officer has commanded a division-sized formation for even a few months. Russell had not only activated the 83d Division; he commanded it at full strength for 14 years and led it to the number one ranking within the Reserve force structure.

At his Army retirement ceremony, he was a given a signed certificate of appreciation from a Regular Army lieutenant general. This was a planned and deliberate slap, not at Russell, but at what he stood for: combat readiness in the U.S. Army Reserve. Decorations such as the Meritorious Service Medal and the Legion of Merit are routinely awarded to retiring lieutenant colonels who have never commanded a unit at all, but Russell was denied even one of these lesser awards. An interesting footnote to all this was the fact that Russell only credited himself with 30 days per year of active duty for pay purposes in all his years of National Guard and Reserve service. General officers in the Guard and the Reserve are authorized to perform up to six months annually of paid active duty, and many routinely do. It was a rare week between 1946 and 1960 that Russell failed to put in the equivalent of two working days on Army business; many weeks he took overnight military trips at his own expense. Yet, his monthly retirement check for 37 years of service, 4 1/2 of them fulltime, 3 1/2 in bitter combat, was around $350 per month. The thought that he was mistreated never seems to have occurred to him. He became, in Reserve retirement, the region's "general emeritus," giving excellent lectures on national security, patriotism, and civil-military relations for all kinds of public occasions.

In the early 1958, Floss and Jack had bought the comfortable family home at 1420 Columbus Avenue, diagonally across the street from the former Ramsey house. Now Russell and Louise realized a real estate dream of their own in 1961 that Louise, especially, had nourished for years, the ownership of a home on the corner of Monroe and Wayne Street. This red brick house, owned before by the Dr. Karl Graefe family, became Louise's project in life. Skilled workmen of all the trades came to the house to improve, to modernize, and to remodel. Further enriching Louise's life was the fact that she and Russell made several trips to England. Louise's personal journal kept on one of these trips reveals a love of Victorian British culture and a knowledge base that could have produced an accurate historical novel.

Floss and Jack added three more children to their family. These were Jack, Jr., 1959; Margot, 1962; and Andrew, 1971. In the early 1960s, Jack left his father's meat packing plant and went into business for himself as a meat broker. For a year he and Floss struggled financially. Russell wanted badly to help his talented son-in-law and represented him legally, until Russell found Jack's career becoming more specialized than his legal background would handle. Jack Waldock's career took off; with Barry Lind he co-founded Lind-Waldock, in 1965, today the world's largest commodity trading firm. Russell, perhaps recalling the days when his own father tried to be a gentleman farmer, read up on pork. His eyes glowed with quiet pride when he shared with friends the dimensions of Jack Waldock's achievements in the commodities world.

"And," he would add, "I don't think I've ever seen a father who was so nuts about his kids.. of course," (here, the shy, boyish grin) "they *are my* grandchildren."

In the early 1960s, Frank Buckingham and Richard Holzaphel added their highly respected names to the law firm of "Ramsey & Didelius," a wonderful association that would endure and add junior partners. Russell was at the peak of his civilian leadership years in the 1960s, but he tried hard to guard some time to spend with each of his grandchildren. Yet his own father's tendency towards stiffness with young family children was also one of his personal traits, making it difficult for him to share spontaneous little moments of joy and discovery. So "Grampy Ramsey and Grammie Louie," as they became known to the family in the 1960s, were sometimes viewed as a slightly distant pair from an earlier age, living out Gothic ideas and forms of life in an era of rapid change and challenge.

Russ and Linda came home from Panama at the end of 1962 to the University of Southern Mississippi, in Hattiesburg, where the Army sent Russ to earn his Master of Arts degree in history. Linda had given birth to Sally in 1961 and was pregnant with Elizabeth, who greeted the world in Hattiesburg in mid 1963. Russell had visited his son's family in Panama in 1962, taking Becky Waldock with him for a grand tour of the Caribbean.

Russell and Louise again visited Russ at Ft. Benning, in 1964, and Russ talked about the impending possibility of military engagement in Vietnam. By mid 1965, Russ was aboard a troop ship commanding a company of paratroop infantry with the 1st Airborne Brigade of the 1st Air Cavalry Division. Russell avidly followed this unaccustomed form of war, fought on a widely dispersed and essentially defensive basis, poring over his son's letters and tapes. The military commander within him knew that a war cannot be won on such terms, and his heart was troubled. In early 1966, he flew to Manila to join Russ for five days of "R & R," and brought with him some of his old battle maps and operations orders from the days when the 37th Division was clobbering units of the Japanese Imperial Army. The father and son soldiers compared tactics used in their respective wars, and, while every ounce of Russell's soul supported his son, he could not bring himself to see that the U.S. military objectives in Vietnam were workable, or even defined. Within a year he advocated the "hit 'em hard one time, arm the South Vietnamese well, and withdraw" strategy that propelled Richard Nixon into the White House in November, 1968.

While Russ was in Vietnam, Floss supported him all the way; she even helped her older girls organize a "support the war" demonstration at Campbell School. But by 1968 she not only advocated withdrawal, as did her father and brother, but actively condemned the war. When Floss and Jack resigned from Grace Episcopal Church, they corresponded cordially with the Bishop, but a regional newspaper made an ugly affair out of it by misquoting Floss in an interview. At the same time, young Russ told his father by telephone one day in 1969 that he was resigning from the Army, and was involved in an ugly confrontation of his own with a Florida Congressman named Bob Sikes. Sorting out all these pieces was tough for a man raised to revere American institutions, and in whose youth the protest over the Ohio State turkey affair was considered radical.

In fact, Russ was teaching R.O.T.C. at the University of Florida in Gainesville; was finishing up his Ph.D. degree in history simultaneously; had been promoted to major; and, shortly before his resignation in June, 1969, discovered that the Army had intended to give him early promotion to lieutenant colonel. But his marriage to Linda was on the rocks, something he could not bear to tell his parents, and he was really exiting the Army in hopes of rescuing a bad marriage with a wife who claimed that her hatred of Army life was the main problem. Russell may have suspected the truth, but then came the Bob Sikes affair- on top of it.

Russ had earned a kind of reputation at the University of Florida for being an "intellectual in uniform" at a time when civilian faculty members were strongly estranged from the Armed Forces. As elected head of a campus committee appointed to study and recommend sweeping changes at the huge and growing university, he was misquoted in a foolish radical newspaper as advocating sexual immorality in the dormitories. Congressman Sikes, an arch conservative Democrat from West Florida cracker country, was also a very senior major general in the Army Reserve, and Vice Chairman of the House Armed Services Committee. Sikes now teed off an "the radical major who advocated shacking up on the campus," demanding his head via court martial. Russell then pulled out his own stops, sending Sikes a strong letter and inducing the Sandusky *Register* to run an article and an editorial that vindicated his son and accused Sikes of being essentially a know-nothing opportunist and a bully.

Coupled with these family incidents of challenge to his values, Russell had to contend with the reality of Louise's increasingly bad health. He discovered the charismatic movement within the Episcopal Church, attended several of their conventions, and joined a group in Sandusky. As his personal life grew more tense and sad, his faith deepened; while he never abandoned the strict trinitarian basis of the Episcopal Church, he believed strongly in faith healing and in miracles sent to those whose faith was strong. Clients who came into Russell's office were sometimes surprised when, after pouring out a sad story and asking for legal support, Russell would ask them to join him in prayer over their particular problems.

Three times his beloved Louise lay at death's door in Good Samaritan Hospital; he organized hundreds of charismatic believers around the country in prayer for her. Floss and Jack visited her often at bedside and thought her recovery unlikely; Russ arrived once from Florida on an emergency call and thought she was already comatose. And a few moments later, as Russell prayed beside her, Russ and a nurse saw Louise awaken, call her son and husband by name, and ask for ice water, always her favorite. If it was not a miracle in fact, no doctor in Sandusky could offer a scientific explanation, and several indeed thought it a divine deliverance.

On May 4, 1970, soldiers of the 37th Division, under authority (but not under control, it turned out) of the Governor of Ohio, fired on student anti-Vietnam War protesters on the campus of Kent State University. The protest was more than that- it had included the burning of the R.O.T.C. Building, rioting, and vandalism- but the deployment of peacekeeping forces was too late, and was horribly bungled. Four students were killed and several more wounded as frightened, mis-directed Guardsmen blazed away; one of those killed was an Army R.O.-T.C student on full scholarship who was on route to class and opposed to the protest. The Guardsmen were tired, having been on strike policing duty in Cleveland for several nights previous to the Kent State affair. They were poorly trained in riot control tactics, many of them being citizen soldiers of personal convenience, serving in the Guard as a way to escape duty in Vietnam.

Ohioans were instantly polarized over the "Kent State Massacre." Pro-Vietnam War citizens felt that all demonstrators were traitors and criminals; some even stated publicly that the student casualties deserved their fate. Anti-Vietnam War citizens felt that the affair represented a repressive government murdering its own citizens to support a wrongful policy. Russell was Sandusky's "general- emeritus," the man who knew about military things, and it was also known that he had served in the 37th Division in World War II. Yet he was a retired Reserve general, not a Guardsman; his position was delicate, no matter what he said.

Russell reviewed films of the Kent State shooting and saw a brigadier general, wearing a helmet and civilian clothes, in the middle of the troops who did the firing; he saw the obviously untrained, out-of-control behavior of the Guardsmen and their leaders; and then he saw the brigadier general simply melt out of the picture and disappear. He was appalled. Later, a politically motivated state review board found little criminal fault in the Guard's actions, even though any Regular Army Court Martial would have convicted many in the chain of command for such a disgraceful performance.

The Kent State affair tore at Russell's heart like few things could do; his own World War II unit had done wrong things, and had been vindicated by civilian politicians who were supposed to demand right things. He came to Norfolk, Virginia, a few days after the affair, to hear Russ give a lecture on Latin American security issues to the resident class at the Armed Forces Staff College, a mixed audience of majors and lieutenant commanders from all the services. A special seminar was assembled for Russell after his son's speech, which, incidentally, had dwelt heavily on such things as riot control by military forces in Latin America. For two solid hours, Russell reiterated for a room filled with professional officers the basic lessons that most Americans had failed to learn and apply in that era. He stressed civilian control of the military, correct federal-state relations, the necessity for troops to be trained, and the absolute demand for integrity among the officer corps. Several times there were tears in his eyes as 50 professional officers learned these lessons from the experience of a citizen soldier who knew and had lived the core values.

Russell and Louise made one last trip to Florida at Christmas, 1973, to see Russ and his family. On their first trip to Gainesville, Russell had gloried in visiting one of Russ's R.O.T.C. class sessions, and had swapped anecdotes with the students. This time, his son was Principal of the Lincoln Vocational Center within the Alachua County Public Schools, and also an elected City Commissioner of Gainesville. Russell felt that his son's life was back on the kind of track that Ramsey men are supposed to follow. He did not know the real condition of his son's marriage, and he and Louise reached a decision.

In early 1974, Russ went to the Gaineswood Condominium, a few blocks from his family home in Gainesville, to let the movers into his parents' new condo. The truck driver rammed into a floodlight in the parking lot, breaking it off, and then, with his partner, jammed the Ramsey family grand piano into the elevator so firmly that the car was out of service all day. Yet when Russell and Louise arrived by car later that day to take up their new residence, their moods were positive; they almost showed a sense of relief about laying down all the burdens they had assumed in Sandusky. To be sure, some of this relief had to do with a new environment, where there were not old friends of half a century who became sick and died off, and there were not scars that brought back unhappiness.

1974 - 1992;
the Gentle General

Sandusky gave Russell and Louise the recognition in 1974, upon their departure, that the Army failed to show in 1964. Good Samaritan Hospital, Grace Church, and several businesses, whose Board of Directors Russell had long served, conducted ceremonies and testimonial banquets. He arrived in Gainesville, in fact, with enough plaques to cover an office wall. But the Gaineswood condominium, which became their final home, was laid out and decorated largely by Louise, who took a whole new lease on life in Florida.

Louise set up the antiques, silver, and art treasures from their Sandusky home in about half the former space, albeit the condo was a 4 bedroom unit with big closets. Their final home became a splendid visual replica of their earlier life, memories adorning the floor space and the walls of each room, beautiful items each having its own story and connection to people important in the memories of these two who seemed to be having a second honeymoon.

Russell and Louise joined the Holy Trinity Episcopal Church in Gainesville; Russell, in earlier times, would have become a Vestry member and, eventually, Junior and Senior Warden. But the retired Russell had different priorities. He became a new kind of knight, a man of service to God and community at an individual and very personal level. Eschewing leadership roles almost with vehemence, Russell delivered altar flowers from the church to the bedside of the sick; he hauled terminal cancer patients to the Shands Teaching Hospital for treatment; he prayed with women who were beaten by their husbands and helped create a shelter house for them. He helped organize St. Francis House for auto and fire accident victims in temporary need of a refuge. He became a kind of institution in a community where humanitarian commitment was practiced and admired, and, while most of the human service centers in Gainesville were secular rather than religious, he got on good working terms with a whole sub-culture of people who help others.

Louise could only move slowly, assisted with a four-legged walker, during the Florida years. So she made her headquarters at the telephone and at her desk, becoming a kind of information center in the lives of the entire family and of friends all across the country. Her address book for those years contains entries from half the states in the nation, and from several foreign countries. She would call Becky Waldock, in Sandusky, and get an update on Laurie, Jack Jr., and Andy, who all lived there still. Then, she would call Beth in Tempe, Arizona, and Margot, in Fayettesville, North Carolina, and give them each a report on the Sandusky tribe. As Ellen, Sally, and Elizabeth Ramsey grew up, she shared details of their lives with zest. Gainesville High School was half a block away, and her Ramsey granddaughters would delight her by dropping by after school. As they began their college years and the moving elsewhere to new lives that followed, she became their news network as well. On her walls she proudly displayed needlepoint pieces which Becky Waldock would make and send to her.

Louise ran a parallel operation to this with her friends, old and new; many a former Sandusky resident had lunch at the Gaineswood condo with Louise and Russell, sharing the table with someone from Gainesville who did similar work or had who had similar interests. Louise's retirement career was people. Her phone calls, her notes and gifts, and her gracious hostessing became the substance of her life with others. And all of this was conducted by a woman who could barely walk, was frequently in great pain, and whose skeleton was paper thin due to the ravages of advanced osteoporosis.

There was also political controversy in the lives of Russell and Louise in their new Florida retreat. Louise initially enjoyed the fact that her son was on the Gainesville City Commission until May, 1976. People would call to complain about garbage service or high utility bills, having dialed the wrong "Russell Ramsey" in the phone book, and get a big pep talk on how good the service really was from the Commissioner's mother. Russell visited often in Russ's schools for troubled youth and acted as a school-parent volunteer link, part of his commitment to personal service. Some of the parents lived deeply troubled lives amid economically wretched circumstances. There was many a colorful incident as some pitiful family, who that very day may have crossed swords with a sheriff's deputy or two, got tangible assistance from a retired Army general, along with prayers.

The Watergate scandal erupted shortly after they arrived in Gainesville. Louise had been an active telephone hustler of votes for Richard Nixon in Sandusky, and now her man was on the ropes. But when President Gerald Ford seemed to be turning things around at the Sesqui-Centennial, she hobbled painfully but happily about at several public events.

At summer's end 1976, there seemed little for Russell and Louise to be cheerful about. They had come to Florida, after all, to spend their final years with their son's family, feeling that they had already spent a rich store of years with their daughter and her six children. But in August, Russ and Linda came in to tell them that they would soon be divorced. To Russell, it must have seemed the final crash in his turbulent family world. So strongly he had yearned for the certainty of that Edwardian era long past, when women stayed at home, men and women stayed married, and people observed social amenities and respected approved social norms without constant challenge and upheaval. This time, it was Louise who was the infantry soldier in the breach, for she persuaded Russell that the thing to do was to support their son's decision, acknowledge the unhappiness that drove his decision, and remain the pillar of stability for all the family members. And that is exactly what she and Russell did for their final years.

Russell drew back, a bit, during this time from his active participation in the charismatic movement, partly because some of the participants exceeded what he thought to be theologically correct. He performed original research, using simultaneous translations of the Scriptures, on such concepts as agape, forgiveness, and salvation. Several of these research projects he reduced to essays which he shared with his Sunday School Class at Holy Trinity Episcopal Church. He and Louise also tried to create ways to do things with their Ramsey granddaughters, to reassure them that the family had not ceased to be. It was a role for which little in life had prepared them, and they rose to the occasion as they rose to the challenges of World War II, unified and adamant in purpose.

At Christmas Eve, 1976, a sickly man who had been an Army private during World War II lay in the Gainesville Veterans Administration Hospital. He had no money, no family, and no friends; he had just been told that he would die fairly soon from inoperable cancer. A white haired gentleman came by his bedside, during the evening, to visit. The gentleman seemed to know about Army things, and about old man things, and they chatted and prayed a bit.

"Say, was you in the Army during the war?" asked the sick man of his visitor.

"Yes," said Russell, "I was overseas quite a while."

"Well, what wuz you?" asked the man.

Gently, Russell answered that he had been an officer, had retired as a major general.

"Well, thanks for comin'," said the veteran. "A general- heck- I never seen nuthin' biggern' a captain when I was in."

In September, 1977, Russell again stood with Russ at the altar of marriage, although Louise was bed-ridden with intestinal adhesions. His new daughter-in-law was the beautiful Roberta Smith from Ocala, Florida, a special education teacher with two sons, Carl, Jr. and Randy, by her own previous marriage. Louise gave Roberta a diamond from the estate of Russell's stepmother, Helen Harten, who had died in 1967, and Roberta designed her own wedding ring to hold the quaintly cut old stone. Russell took Roberta to a couple of his final charismatic Christianity conventions. When Roberta's father, W. Robert Smith, the retired City Attorney of Ocala, passed away unexpectedly, Russell and Louise attended the graveside services, and they forged a warm friendship with Roberta's mother Lois.

In 1978 Roberta arranged for Susie Gilley, sister of a teacher at Russ's Alternative School, to work for Russell and Louise as housekeeper. As they aged, she progressively took on a trusted role as their personal caregiver.

On July 1, 1979, Roberta delivered Russell Robert Ramsey, the "Russell" making him the fourth in the Ramsey sequence, the "Robert" for Roberta's father. Perhaps primogeniture has passed away as a political feature in western civilization, but any grandparent still cherishes a grandson who bears the family's male lineal given name. Bobby Ramsey became a special, late-in-life pal to his Grammie and Grampy Ramsey.

When Roberta gave her new father-in-law a copy of her Ph.D. dissertation in special education at the University of Florida, "Grampy" Ramsey was probably the only person outside her faculty committee and her husband who read it cover-to-cover, cherished its contents, and discussed it with her. And Russell's Gainesville friends were proudly shown his new necktie which included Roberta's two sons on the roster of twelve grandchildren. When people would sometimes want to pursue details about who was a step-grandchild, and who was a child by which marriage, Russell's eyes would tighten up a bit, and he would reply, "I have an even dozen grandchildren, and I love them all."

An unexpected dividend for Russell and Louise in those last years was the arrival of six great-grandchildren, four of whom they saw personally, with the last two on the way when Russell died. Russell used to joke that God must have intended him to have only granddaughters when the first three offspring of each of his own children were girls. The gender pendulum swung hard over, for all eight of his great-grandchildren were boys.

Floss's daughter Beth brought her two boys, Dustin and Daniel, to Gainesville from Tempe, Arizona for visits. Beth's sister Margot had two little boys as well, Ian and Erik; Russell and Louise met them on a trip to Fayetteville, North Carolina, where the boys' father was stationed with the U.S. Air Force. Jack Waldock, Jr. had a son who continued the given name of his father and paternal grandfather. Known as "John Henry," he spent his baby and toddler years fighting for life against a terrifying immunity deficiency. Russell and Louise prayed constantly for this child to the end of their days, and they came to adore his beautiful mother Jill as she and Jack, Jr. struggled heroically to help their son survive. Russ's daughter Sally gave birth to Eric Price on the last day of 1989, and Andy Waldock celebrated the arrival of little Andrew shortly after Russell's death. Finally, Roberta's son Carl Jr. and wife Susan were expecting little Carl, IVth, when Russell died; the boy was born just a few weeks afterwards and became known as "Jay."

There were two final disappointments in Russell's life. The first was that Russ, Roberta, and Bobby moved to Albany, Georgia in January, 1982, when Russ was made Director of the huge Turner Job Corps Center. Russell and Louise had surrendered their Sandusky life to take up the new one in Gainesville, Florida, near their son, so this career happenstance might have been ill received; but Russell and Louise gave the move their positive and sincere blessings, doing all that was possible to make the transition easy. The second tribulation- declining health and mobility, coupled with falls and other medical emergencies- not only made life difficult, but also limited them to just three brief visits to Albany, and virtually ended the trips they loved so much.

The Ronald Reagan White House years brought joy to Louise's political heart; she felt that the country was once again getting its values in order. Russell lamented the enormity of the public spending in the Reagan years, but in the back of his mind was the time in 1942, at San Francisco, when Ron Reagan had enthusiastically pitched in his acting services to entertain the men of the 37th Division, en route to battle in the Pacific. Russell and Louise, in the 1980s, gloried in their visits from the Sandusky side of the family; several times they engineered family occasions by getting Russ and Roberta to bring Bobby down from Albany while Floss and some of her offspring were in town.

For Russell, the beginning of the end came with the breakdown of microscopic capillaries which nourish the brain with blood, a condition called ischemia. He made a trip, in 1984, to Howe Military School in Indiana to receive the Distinguished Alumnus Award. Floss, Laurie, and Andy came over from Sandusky to be with him, and he probably exaggerated his ability to cope with a long trip. So, a few months later, Russell and Louise made what was to be their last big trip, going by automobile to Fayetteville, North Carolina, to visit with Floss's daughter Margot and her husband, and to meet Margot's two little boys. Russell suffered a severe ischemiatic attack during the trip. He was hospitalized at Ft. Bragg's Womack Army Hospital for several days. When he returned to Gainesville, he never really recovered. Subsequent attacks would result in blacking out and falling; then there would be a period of hospitalization when he could not care for himself. The outcome of each attack was loss of memory, impairment of leg movement, dizziness, and diminished energy. As the neurological impairments worsened, Louise had mounting problems as well: intestinal adhesions, a terrible fall that resulted in the implantation of a teflon-coated metal hip, and horrible lower back pain that never stopped. Gamely they fought on, each letting family members know that he or she would care for the other until the end.

Louise suffered a bad fall at the beginning of 1990, and, following hospital repairs, was allowed to come home. She was totally bed-bound, now, and in continuous agony. Her beloved Russell sat in his chair in the study, three rooms down the hall, watching television, occasionally trying to read large print books, and wondering constantly about what was the matter with his mind. When blood flowed properly in the capillaries, he could reason, and his memory of things long past was amazing; but details of recent events eluded him. Louise, for her part, lamented strongly her inability to care for Russell.

On July 12, 1990, Russell stared in disbelief as an ambulance team wheeled Louise out the door for her final trip to the hospital. Her vital signs were falling fast, and her intestinal tract was blocked with an adhesion. Desperate, high risk surgery was done, and, for a few hours, she cheated death again. Then, in the early morning hours of July 13, she became conscious for a short while, spoke gratefully to the assistant rector from Holy Trinity Episcopal Church, lapsed into unconsciousness, and died.

Most of the family assembled for the memorial service at Holy Trinity Episcopal Church. Bobby Ramsey sang the "*Pie Jesu*" from Gabriel Faure's *Requiem* in a flute-like soprano voice, touching hearts unforgettably. A second memorial service, with hundreds in attendance, was held for Louise in Grace Episcopal Church, in Sandusky; Russell, of course, was much too feeble to make this trip but gloried in the videotape of the service which Floss showed him. Russell was staggered but courageous following the loss of his beloved companion of 61 years. At times, his memory lapses were merciful, for they reduced the periods of time for him to grieve helplessly for his departed "Louie." For a few weeks he was cared for at his condo by shift nurses, but in late September he went to a nursing care facility in Gainesville.

Doctors felt that Russell could not last long. But as his mobility failed, so too, did his breathing, his memory, and his internal body functions. He needed regular, hands-on care, and most of the time his mind was active enough to know who he was, and to recall much of his earlier life. So on October 31st, 1990, Russ drove his father north to Albany, Georgia, there to stay in a nursing home, with loving staff to bring him out to the family home and to Sunday church services when he felt well enough to go.

Russell's final sixteen weeks of life in Albany were a lesson to all who saw him on how a Christian knight exits the world. Albany is a pro-military city, and Operation Desert Shield coincided almost exactly with Russell's short tenure there. He met several National Guardsmen en route to mobilization and gave them little tips for success. On a cold morning in November, 1990, he sat at the curb in his wheelchair as the Albany National Guard unit paraded down the street to leave town for battle training, just half a century after he did the same thing in Sandusky. He fought off the mental confusion that overcame him as he met each new person, concentrating on the face, struggling to remain in the present, and saying memorable, quotable things to many people.

On Sunday, February 18, 1991, he was to have heard Russ sing Fanny Crosby's rousing solo "Open the Gates of the Temple" in church, but he was too sick even to let himself be dressed. So on Monday, Dr. Paul Luthman, Pastor of Covenant Presbyterian Church where the family attends, brought Russell a tape of his son's performance to hear in bed at the nursing home. Russ, by chance, was there. Russell could hardly speak, but his lips formed the words, and he whispered a few lines. He watched Russ's face intently and completely understood what was going on.

The next night, Roberta stopped by his bedside after teaching her master's students at Albany State College. She read him several verses of his favorite Scripture, which had become their evening custom. When she finished, she said, "Good night, Grampy, I'll see you tomorrow." He said, simply, "Good-bye," but he hugged her hard and did not want to let go.

"No, Grampy, it's just 'Good night'," she said. "I'll see you in the morning."

He smiled faintly and repeated, "Good-bye."

At dawn, the morning nurse was unable to awaken him. He was taken to the hospital, where all revival measures were tried without success, and, by breakfast time, his heart stopped. To all the medical and nursing staff who worked with him, those final weeks in the room with the U.S. and two-star general's flags on staffs at his bedside, it appeared that he accepted God's call to join his beloved Louise when he closed his eyes the previous evening.

Shortly before Russell's death, vandals had burned the Holy Trinity Episcopal Church in Gainesville, leaving little but a gutted shell. He was never told of this event, but, at his memorial service in another church nearby, over 150 people came out on a cold, rainy morning to honor his memory. Much of his family assembled again at Grace Episcopal Church in Sandusky, the next week, for a second and final memorial service. Floss spoke eloquently of his service to God and country; Roberta shared the final Scripture she had read with him; Russ and Bobby sang Mendelssohn's "Hear My Prayer/Oh, for the Wings of a Dove," which Russell had heard his son perform 45 years ago, from the same choir bench. Russell and Louise both donated their bodies to science at the Shands Teaching Hospital in Gainesville. Floss arranged for the urns containing their ashes to repose side-by-side in the Collombarium at Grace Church in Sandusky. Memorials to them both poured in to charitable and religious institutions for over a year after their deaths.

What Manner of Man?

Russell A. Ramsey left about one hundred pages of hand written and home typed speeches and research summaries in an old fashioned cardboard storage box once used for legal documents. It was buried under clutter in a bureau drawer, along with some photographs taken with his mother and father when he was a young boy; only Floss and his sister Jean had ever seen the photographs, many years ago, and no one even knew the existence of the documents. The few times that it was even possible to raise the question of publishing his written work, or of doing a biography, he quickly squashed the notion.

"No one wants to read that kind of thing," he would say. "They can find my career in the Princeton *Alumni Magazine*." If he was, in fact, a perfect example of the lawyer and the citizen soldier in his time, living these roles as James Madison, Thomas Jefferson, John Jay, and Alexander Hamilton envisioned them when the Republic began, then it is fair to evaluate. Did he hit the mark? And where did he miss the mark?

The didactic role of his father, and of the schools he attended, cannot be overemphasized in his life. Russell K. Ramsey, Howe Military School, Princeton University, and Michigan Law School provided Russell with a thorough, substantive understanding of American law and Constitutional precedents, and of the citizen's role and obligations in the national defense process. The cultural period in which he lived was rich in patriotic hoop-la, and masculine assertion, but also with a positive and conscious sense of mission. Manifest destiny on the American frontier was closing when Russell was born; America's role as regional and then world superpower was fast rising. On the domestic scene, the cultural fabric was a mixture of British Edwardianism and U.S. Progressivism; these were both a blessing and a burden in Russell's life. Russell's culture kept him ever seeking the best, striving to go upward and onward to worthy service; but it suppressed honest human emotion and interpersonal sensitivity.

The women in Russell's life form a complex mosaic of joy and tragedy. His loving and lovable mother was made almost a saint and a martyr in his eyes, especially when her death was linked thoughtlessly by family members to the process of his birth. His step-mother gave him female tenderness and joy, and so, too, did his adopted sister; but these women were both kept at a distance from him during much of his life by the powerful presence of his beloved wife, who, in his eyes, could do no wrong. He gloried in his friendship with his daughter, but when she was weighted down with six children and a fast-changing national values system, he sometimes found it hard to be close with her too. His first daughter-in-law never grew close to him at all, although he tried to let her, and she betrayed him in his eyes by refusing to love his son; his second daughter-in-law brought him great joy, but entered his life when he was already old and sick. To her was granted the gift of fulfilling earlier wonders of female companionship in the late December of life.

One suspects that Russell was a better father to his son than his own father was to him. Yet the long war years, the demanding leadership years in Sandusky, and his psychological inability to do relaxed little things with children made it such that his son could only know intimately the full glory of his person when he was an old man.

What about his career, where he was seen by others as a man of steely integrity, great intellect, and hard drive? Could he have been a U.S. Senator? Might he have risen to three- or four-star rank had he been a career Army officer? Or even in the Reserve, had he been willing to stroke the political system? It is tempting to conclude that Russell could have risen to almost any height in life, had he not been burdened with his wife's emotional and health troubles during his key career years. But there is a deeper philosophical issue which counter argues this notion.

America does not elevate people from the ranks of the near-famous to the top of the mountain for the kinds of leadership traits that took Russell so far. His forte, first, last, and always, lay in perfect accomplishment of tough assignments- winning legal briefs that others could not write, movement orders for huge troop units that succeeded when other men's work failed, hospital service plans that won huge federal grants against stiff odds- these were his professional championships in life. He was not good at all at such necessary political tasks as rousing speeches that bring people to one's cause on an emotional basis. His best speeches were great because they were clear and didactic, not rousing. His best exercises in human power relationships lay in persuading higher authorities that some vital task could be done, not in exacting a political payoff in return for his support. While he admired some politicians, he was distrustful of the genre, and to some degree of the political process, itself.

No, Russell A. Ramsey reached the exact pinnacle in life that his God commanded him to achieve. He contributed legal and institutional leadership to one Ohio city that benefitted greatly from his presence. He led men in battle in a variety of settings that won the objectives with the least casualties. He supported evolving civic and defense institutions in Cold War America with excellence, quality, and intelligence, never with flamboyance of the sort that might result in thousands of people calling upon him to run for high office. And when he was older, he gave richly of his knighthood to another city in Florida, and to his family as they passed through tumultuous years of change with many hard falls.

He was a man called by God to be more than ordinary men. He answered this call fully within the talents given to him. He defended law and country with courage, dignity, persistence, and honor. Russell A. Ramsey answered the call of James Madison and Thomas Jefferson to the rule of law over the whim of men, and to the defense of the Republic by its best prepared citizens. He did it in a tradition that evolved from late medieval

Christian knighthood. This life was knighthood personified in 20th century America.

Russell and his mother Florence in 1912

Russell with stepmother Helen, in 1915,
at the Columbus Avenue house

Russell in uniform of Battalion Adjutant,
Cadet Lieutenant, Howe Military School, Indiana,
with his father Russell K.

Russell's sister Jean
poses atop her pony at the
Lake Erie House, 1923

Russell, Louise, and baby Floss
at the Lake Erie house, 1931

Russell with little Russ
at the Columbus Avenue house in 1938.
Behind them, the Studebaker sedan in which they went
to Florida in 1939.

Russell receives the Legion of Merit from Maj. Gen. Robert S. Beightler, Commanding General, 37th Infantry Division, on Bougainville, Solomon Islands, 1943.

Russell and Louise
at the Columbus Avenue house, in 1949

**Russell and Louise
on vacation in Pinehurst, North Carolina, 1958**

On Law and Country 89

Russell R., Russell W., Russell A., and (inset from portrait), Russell K. Ramsey, Gainesville, 1988

Maj. Gen. Russell A. Ramsey
U.S. Army Reserve 1904 - 1991

BATTLE FOR IRISAN BRIDGE
August 1945

For more than two months, the Japanese had been fighting a stubborn, skillful delaying action on the western and southern approaches to Baguio, Luzon, Philippine Islands. The few roads and trails leading to the Philippine summer capital were ideally suited for determined and prolonged defensive action. Winding torturously through the mountains, each rise dominated by a succession of high ridges, shoulders dropping off precipitously on one side and rising at 80 degree angles on the other, these routes confined and canalized the attacker. Enemy riflemen and machine gunners, holed up for suicidal stands at each strategic twist and turn, inflicted casualties on the point squads of the advancing columns before the man-moles could be found and fixed. Whole regiments, moving along in route column formation, were held up while assault teams burned, smoked, dug, or blasted out the Japanese. Still, the returns in killed Nipponese were small. The enemy was expending himself, but in twos and threes.

Japanese artillery was particularly accurate and effective. Flat trajectory 47 millimeter and 75 millimeter mountain guns plastered the main body of troops from the dominant ridges and sporadically dumped shells into supply and command post installations. Set deep in the wooded hills, well camouflaged, and firing at irregular intervals, these pieces defied detection. They shot down the throats of the advancing troops with a nerve-wracking unpredictability throughout the entire campaign. The ubiquitous 90 millimeter mortar, fired from wooded draws and registered on the twists and turns, harassed the columns. Their wink muzzle blast made detection by artillery and cub aircraft observers extremely difficult. The Japanese understood the defensive possibilities of the Baguio area, and they were well supplied with ammunition and supplies laid up in better days. Although pushed back and overrun, they exacted a high price for each one hundred yards.

In spite of the obstacles, the attacking Americans drove inexorably forward. On 13 April, 1945, the 148th Infantry regiment, fresh from a month of rest following its 137 mile march to Manila and its combat successes there, was committed to the fight. The 37th Division had the mission of moving up the Baguio-Naguilian Road (Highway 9) on the western approaches to Baguio, and of eventually capturing the summer capital. Meeting the same stubborn Japanese resistance, this Regiment ground steadily ahead, supported by tanks, tank destroyers, artillery, and engineer demolition crews. By 17 April, the drive forward had reached the last important bend in the road, 200 yards from the vital Irisan River Bridge and the sign on its far end "Baguio City Limits". That bridge had been demolished by the Japanese days earlier.

Intensive patrol activity indicated that the enemy realized the strategic importance of the bridge. Whatever the cost, the Americans must be kept from rebuilding it and from crossing the river at the point. Here, at last, the Americans discovered Japanese in large numbers. They noted well-prepared defensive positions on all of the key terrain features, positions that were well-manned and heavily gunned by a fanatical defender who knew that when the Irisan Bridge and its surrounding hills fell, then too, fell Baguio. Of all the natural defensive positions in the Baguio mountains, the ones covering the Irisan were the most ominous. The bridge itself was in a valley, surrounded by eight distinct ridges and resembling a drop of water in a tea cup with the bridge being the drop and the high ground, the rim. These ridges were all defended, were mutually supporting, and yet any one could be held independent of the others. The terrain was heavily wooded and the minor trails leading to the Japanese positions were few, narrow, steep, and of course, well covered by automatic fire. A stretch of road, approximately 200 yards on either side of the bridge, could be swept by machine gun and rifle fire from any of the eight ridges, and the flat trajectory artillery, concealed in caves and dragged out for special occasions, could pound any remunerative targets within this 400 yard zone. The 90 millimeter mortars were registered in on the bridge and surrounding areas, and the American commanders agreed that any attempt to enter this no-man's land without first conquering the eight ridges would be suicidal.

On 17 April, spearheaded by tanks from Company B, 775th Tank Battalion, leading elements of the 148th Infantry Regiment consisting of Company G and Company F started around this last curve before the Irisan Bridge. The First Platoon of Company F attacked Ridge A from the west, and Company G attacked astride the Highway, supported by a platoon of tanks, a platoon of M7 self-propelled 105mm howitzers, and a platoon of M18 Tank destroyers. Rifle and machine gun fire greeted Company G, and 47 millimeter fire narrowly missed the lead tank, causing it to back up and shift its firing position. As the tank backed up, it rolled off the side of the narrow road and fell down the steep cliff, rolling end over end until it hit the bottom, 50 yards down. A patrol from Company G clambered down the cliff to rescue the tank crew, and their appearance was timely as the Japanese had dispatched a patrol of their own to finish off any of the crew yet alive. Our men routed the Japanese and brought back four of the five man crew. The fifth man was dead, but the other four, badly shaken and bruised, would live. At 1120 hours, the Regimental Commander came forward to plan the next move around the bend in the road. At 1130 hours, the Japanese pulled one more trick out of their threadbare bag. Two enemy tanks, one medium and one light, came racing around this bend toward our column, from a position of hiding. As they straightened out they fired 47 millimeter and 50 caliber guns wildly at the American troops on either side of the narrow road. Behind each tank on specially constructed platforms were twelve rifleman, also blazing away, and the lead tank had mines placed on its front with the intention of ramming our tanks and setting off the mines. This intention was effectuated and one of our own tanks had its tread torn off by the collision and ensuing explosion. Within ten minutes, the enemy tanks were knocked out by our own tank fire, and the enemy riflemen were annihilated by our own riflemen. However, the surprise attack resulted in moderate casualties, to our forces, including the Regimental Commander who was hit badly in the right leg. A combat patrol of one platoon of Company G supported by tanks was immediately sent around the bend to check on further Japanese tricks, and this patrol again encountered intense machine gun and rifle fire from the ridges. More casualties were suffered, but were pulled out heroically under fire by aid men and by their own comrades. The patrol reported that no more tanks were lurking around the bend, and then, under order, withdrew. The battle of the Irisan Bridge had begun, and was destined to end five days later with the annihilation of a reinforced Battalion of yellow fanatics and the breaking of the back of the Japanese defenses around Baguio.

At 1300 hours, Company F was ordered to seize the high ground (Ridge A) north of Highway 9 (see enclosed sketch), and Company G's mission was to proceed astride Highway 9, supported by tanks. Heavy fire stopped Company G's advance, and the lead platoon of Company F was met by withering machine gun fire as it climbed up Ridge A. Engaging the enemy in a fierce fire fight, this platoon was able to divert the Japanese long enough for the other two rifle platoons of Company F to move to the right and left rear of the enemy. Just prior to darkness, the three platoons had closed in on the enemy defenses, and the forty-six Japanese holding the ridge were annihilated. Quickly organizing the company for defense, the company commander of Company F anticipated a night attack. When it came in the form of a banzai charge, three squads of Nipponese were cut down by the crossfire of two well placed Browning automatic Rifles.

The First Battalion, meanwhile, had the mission of patrolling and securing the trails leading north to the towns of Philippine and Trinidad to cut the lines of reinforcements and supplies. First Battalion patrols continually bumped into Japanese patrols trying to return to the Irisan area. These patrols were aggressively engaged whenever found and on the 17th of April, an estimated company of Nipponese was attacked by a reinforced platoon from Company A, after a heavy artillery preparation, and was forced to retire from the clash leaving behind fifteen of their ancestor-bound comrades.

On 18 April, a daring two-pronged thrust was decided by the American commanders. The Second Battalion was to continue the attack to the north of the highway and seize the next higher ground, Ridge B, which controlled the draw leading directly to the bridge. The Third Battalion was ordered to attack and occupy the high ground, Ridges C, D, and E, to the south of the road. The Third Battalion objective was to be taken by a very wide end-run sweep across the Irisan River, down the steep wooded draws, ending up behind the enemy defenses, which were obviously facing the bridge. The attack was supported by heavy direct fire from one platoon of M7s and one platoon of M18s from Company B, 637th Tank Destroyer Battalion. This bold move tested not only the fighting efficiency of the men, but even more, their physical condition, for the terrain was practically impassable. It appeared impassable to the Japanese also, for the attack, which jumped off at 0830 hours, proceeded without enemy opposition until Ridge C was reached. The Japanese were taken by surprise, and offered only light resistance on Ridge C. Several pressed the inevitable hand grenade to honorable stomach, and the rest of the defenders were either killed or driven off into the gorge separating Ridge C from Ridge E. By 1240 hours, the Third Battalion had secured Ridge C. The Second Battalion ran into stiffer enemy resistance, since the surprise factor was missing. Company E, in the lead, was plastered by machine gun, mortar, and artillery fire from the top of Ridge B, where an estimated 150 Japanese fanatics were making their last stand. Stopped cold by this fire, Company E reorganized while our artillery was laid down on the ridge. Then, attacking in the late afternoon, Company E won half of Ridge B by nightfall. This half was the lower half of the ridge, and during the night, the men were subjected to intense direct fire from all the weapons in the

Japanese repertoire. Our own artillery answered, but the Japanese countered with well organized infiltration tactics which were repulsed only after vicious hand to hand combat. One soldier in a perimeter foxhole with two buddies saw a Japanese hand grenade fall into his hole. Without hesitation he jumped on the grenade with both feet, mashed it partially into the ground, and then stood on it until it exploded. He lost a leg but his two comrades were uninjured.

On the 19th, a heavy air strike was directed against Ridges F and G, and then after an artillery preparation, Company E, reinforced by Company G, continued the assault. The Japanese, who had holed up during the air and artillery strikes, came out of their caves when the strikes lifted and fought bitterly. Inching forward, a machine gun squad from Company E was able to break through the Nipponese defenses and emplace the light machine gun on high ground on the north flank of Ridge B. Although two of the machine gunners were killed by desperate Japanese counter-attackers, the remainder of the squad held the ground long enough for more soldiers to come through the gap and support the spear-heading machine gun. This breakthrough so diverted the Japanese that one platoon from Company G was able to reach the south flank of Ridge B, and at 1700 hours, a coordinated attack was launched from the front, the right, and the left. Elements of two rifle companies, moving ahead with wild yells and firing accurately from their hips completely overran the Japanese positions and by nightfall the Ridge was secure.

The Third Battalion, from vantage points on Ridge C, covered by rifle, machine gun, and mortar fire the emplacements on Ridges D and E (Chocolate Drop Hill). Our supporting 105 howitzers joined the crowd for thirty minutes, massaging those features thoroughly. After this preparation, Company I passed through Company K and secured Ridge D. Then, using both C and D as a base of fire, Ridge E was pounded heavily and Company L, moving to the left rear of Company I suddenly veered to the left and charged up Ridge E. This Hill's organized defenses had been pulverized, and it was secured after six snipers were killed, four of whom were cut in two by a veteran Browning automatic rifle team from the Third Platoon of Company L. The attack on Chocolate Drop Hill was clearly observed from Ridge C and represented textbook portrayal of small unit tactics. Moving through the heavy terrain, a reinforced squad, approached to within fifteen yards of the Chocolate Drop unnoticed. The Sergeant Squad Leader deployed his men using hand and arm signals, and the observers on Ridge C anxiously watched the enemy defenders who were scanning the approaches but evidently overlooking this deployed squad because of the dense underbrush. Spread out in a skirmish line and moving cautiously, the squad reached the top of the hill. One of the enemy suddenly noticed a soldier with a Browning automatic rifle ten yards away. Sad Sakomoto threw up his hands and yelled, and this cry, intended as a warning to his comrades, inspired a spontaneous American charge. One of the Japanese, lying on his belly with field glasses to his eyes, was killed just as he turned around to see what the yelling was about. The rest of the enemy, 25 in number, were hit so stunningly by 15 of our soldiers that they fired a total of only eight shots before they were killed. Not one man in our attacking force was wounded, and the Japanese were liquidated.

By the evening of the 19th, the Japanese controlled only Ridges F, G, and H. However, every last egg was in these three baskets, and it was expected that this Hill Mass of F, G, and H would be the strongest defended position yet encountered. The First Battalion was relieved of its security and patrol mission on the 19th, and it was decided to pass the First Battalion through the Second Battalion for the big attack on these last obstacles. At 0840 hours, 20 April, the First Battalion jumped off after preparatory air strikes and artillery shelling. Company C moved up the slope on the right toward Ridge F, and Company A advanced on the left toward Ridge G. Company B was in reserve. Company C moved up the slope on the right toward Ridge F and Company A advanced on the left toward Ridge G. Company B was in reserve. Company C met moderate resistance in its ascent but Company A was hard hit by machine gun and rifle fire. At 1000 hours, Company C had reached the top of its ridge, still against moderate resistance, then turned to the flank of the Japanese positions holding up Company A. This enfilade fire speedily disorganized the defenders, and by 1130 hours, the top of the Ridge G was also in our hands. On the reverse slope of the hill, however, there were strong enemy forces, well dug-in, and our troops on the ridge were shot at when they maneuvered over the crest. Knee mortar shells dropped in the area, and when a large patrol was sent around the side to eliminate this threat, it was smothered with intense machine gun and rifle fire. One platoon of Company B, at the bottom of the ridge, was then ordered to clean out this opposition. Led by a veteran Technical Sergeant who soon afterwards received his direct commission, this platoon followed the path taken by Company C on the right flank. About halfway up the ridge, the platoon veered sharply to the right, and moved the long way around the side of Ridge F to the opposite slope which brought them directly BELOW the enemy positions on Ridge G's high reverse slope. These "Hardway" tactics caught the Japanese unawares, and the Platoon Sergeant expertly deployed his men on a firing line and when deployed, gave the order to open fire. After five minutes of intense small arms fire, he led his men up the hill, still firing, and without losing a man, the platoon reached the Japanese positions, and mopped up the few Nipponese still alive. 15 Japanese were killed in this minor action, and eleven of them had bullet holes in their backs or the backs of their heads, attesting to the surprise element of the exhausting American maneuver.

90 millimeter mortar fire caused casualties during the afternoon and evening while elements of the battalion were cleaning the enemy out of caves and dugouts which dotted the hills. Other elements planned strong defensive positions in expectation of an enemy counterattack that night. However, the Japanese, contrary to our assumption, wouldn't wait. At 1235 hours fifty enemy riflemen and machine gunners, steadily approaching up the draw between Ridge G and F, were discovered by a two man

Browning automatic rifle team standing outpost duty near Company A Command Post. Without hesitation they both stood straight up to get a better field of fire and poured two clips of Browning automatic rifle bullets into the enemy. One of the two was killed and the other was hit in the chest and knocked to the ground. Still conscious, he feigned death until the Japanese group moved to within five feet of him and the opened fire once again, killing several more and forcing the rest to take temporary cover. By that time, the First Sergeant of Company A, hearing the firing, had rounded up 28 men, including the supply sergeant, two radio men, the communications sergeant, the assistant company clerk, and two depleted rifle squads resting near the CP, and the 29 men joined the lone Browning automatic rifleman. Without hesitation, these reinforcements, whooping and hollering, pounced on the larger force of Japanese, killed 30 of them and made the remainder run for their lives back down the draw. Between 1630 hours and 1730 hours, the Japanese made two attempts to retake Company C's Ridge F, but both attempts were decisively repulsed. Mortar and artillery fire fell into the perimeters during the night, but no Japanese counterattack materialized. The Japanese had evidently expended their banzai men in the three abortive attacks that day. Licking their wounds, what was left of them, retreated to Ridge H, the last bit of the defensive rim around the Irisan River Bridge. There they waited for the inevitable American drive the next day.

At 0800 hours, 21 April 1945, after a thirty minute artillery barrage, Company B and C moved against Ridge H. Meeting resistance from a badly mauled enemy, Company C reached and occupied the southern portion of Ridge H by 1200 hours. Company B passed through Company C and occupied the northern portion of the ridge by 1400 hours. 182 dead were counted on Ridge H alone, about half of them the victims of the incessant artillery, mortar, and air support, and the other half dug out by riflemen hell-bent on finishing this dirty job. Extensive patrolling by all three battalions in the surrounding draws and hills uncovered isolated enemy pockets which were carefully mopped up. A combat patrol of one platoon from Company I proceeding from the south end of Ridge D to the bridge on the highway closed six large caves with demolitions and captured one 75 millimeter mountain gun and four 47 millimeter anti-tank guns, and killed 26 of the enemy. The engineers began work on a bypass across the Irisan as soon as Ridge H was secured, and by 1800 hours, vehicles, including medium tanks, were able to cross. The 129th Infantry Regiment, on the 22nd of April, was ordered to pass through the 148th and this move was effected without incident.

The 129th Regiment then attacked the Japanese in the direction of Trinidad. Although the fighting was still bitter, the Japanese were disorganized and they soon joined their relatives and friends in the Shinto Heaven. This screening force enabled other infantry regiments to move into Baguio after brushing aside last-ditch defenders on the outskirts on the town. It was obvious however, that when the engineer corporal drove home the last nail on the wooden by-pass across the Irisan he was also driving home the last nail on the coffin of Japanese defenses around the Philippine summer capital.

In breaking the back of the Japanese defenses during this five day struggle around the Irisan, the regiment killed a total of 430 counted enemy soldiers. Our losses were one officer and 33 enlisted men killed in action or died of wounds, 12 officers and 132 enlisted men wounded in action and eight enlisted men injured, mainly sprained ankles sustained in the arduous ups and downs of the valleys and ridges. Thousands of rounds of artillery and mortar ammunition were captured. In addition, two 75 millimeter guns, four 47 millimeter guns, and numerous machine guns, rifles, and other equipment were taken.

The feats of heroism evinced by the men of the regiment were legion. Based on this five-day action alone, the following awards had been recommended, some posthumous: 6 Distinguished Service Crosses; 48 Silver Stars; and 93 Bronze Stars.*(2) In many other cases the teamwork and efficiency of squads and platoons were illustrious, but the business-like ease with which the missions were accomplished precluded acts of gallantry.

The battle for the Irisan may not have been the most heroic or the most brilliant single action of the Pacific War, but it was an uncommon feat of arms, combining the elements of aggressiveness, sound tactics, courage, and skill which are the criterion for superiority in the infantry.

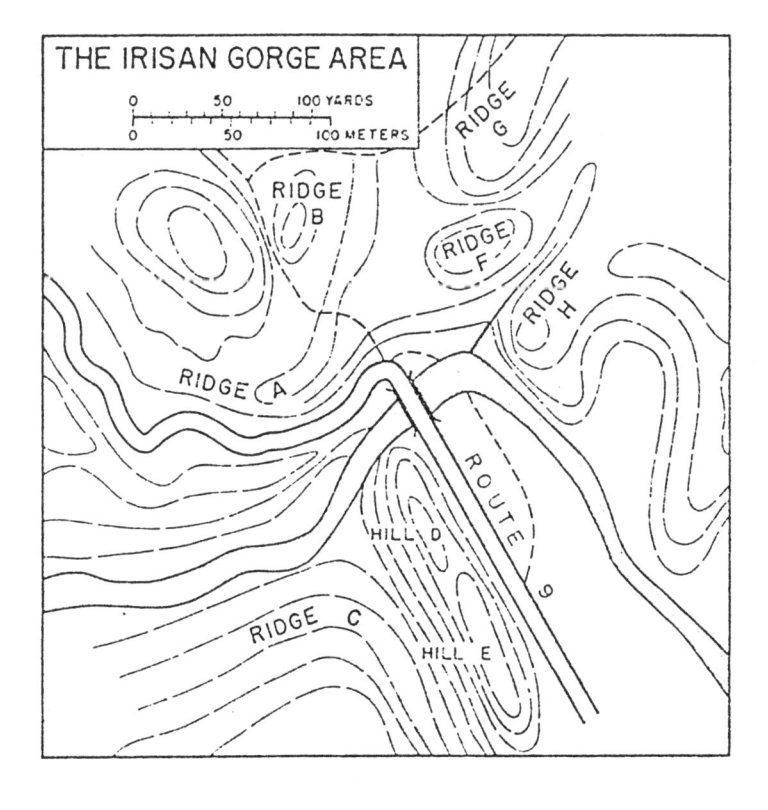

Sketch of Irisan area

DAUGHTERS OF THE AMERICAN REVOLUTION
Sandusky, September 7, 1956

Once upon a time, as the story books say, there were but two persons upon the face of the earth, and if we take the story literally, the second one arrived some time after the first. Adam needed no law books to guide him in the business of getting along with others. There were no others. But with the coming of Eve, the world's population doubled- and all the rest of the story involves the human race.

Please do not interpret what I have said as an indication that trouble came with Eve. I suspect the troubles would have been greater, although perhaps different, if the second arrival had been a man. Certain it is that the next two inhabitants of this earth were men- Cain and Abel, and you know what happened to them.

Law is a set of rules by which people who live together must be governed in order to reduce the frictions of human intercourse. It must be enforced or it is not law. In a state of nature, each man is free to get along as best he can. If, however, he chooses to congregate with others, he must pay something for the privilege of this association. The price is some part of his former freedom to do as he pleases. Historically, law has often been simply the will of a strong man, who remains in power until he is overthrown by a stronger force. Fortunately for us, our ancestors decided as early as the days of King John- in 1215- that the power of the crown should be limited by a set of fundamental rules governing property and life, and this decision, known as Magna Carta, has been the basic governmental philosophy of the English speaking peoples. It is the foundation of the English constitution, and is the foundations of American law, the principal difference being that the English constitution is unwritten and traditional, whereas the United States Constitution is written. In substance, both constitutions are based upon consent of the governed.

Many generations later, some thirteen groups of people living along the eastern seaboard of America, joined together in common cause and cast off the reins of British government. This left them without government- thirteen little colonies adrift on the shores of the great American continent, beset by all the dangers of nature and the Indians, impoverished by the cost of a long war, and exposed to the peril of invasion by any avaricious nation in the world. Fortunately, disagreements on the European continent provided our thirteen little groups of people with the time in which to build some fences. The first fence was united action against a future invader. Therefore, the now free colonies decided to band together for defense against the outsider, and to promote free and equitable relations between themselves. Accordingly, conferences were held, and a written document was produced which became effective in 1781. Known as the Articles of Confederation, this is a curious instrument. Let us look at it for a moment:

Article 1: "The style of this confederacy shall be The United States of America.

Article 3: The said States hereby severally enter into a firm league of friendship with each other, for their common defenses, the security of their liberties, and their mutual and general welfare, binding themselves to assist each other, against all force offered to, or attacks made upon them, or any of them, on account of religion, sovereignty, trade, or any other pretence whatever.

Article 6: ****** No state shall engage in any war without the consent of the United States in Congress assembled unless such state be actually invaded by enemies ******.

Article 8: ****** Provides that all the cost of war shall be born by the several states in proportion to the value of the lands and buildings in each state.

Article 9: Provides for an interim committee to sit between meetings of Congress, called "a committee of the states."

This is not a history book, and therefore I will not discuss the events of American history which soon proved the unworkability of this league of friendship, a mere treaty between states. In passing, however, it is worth recalling that it was under the seal of the Confederate Congress, affixed July 13, 1787, that the Ordinance for the Government of the Territory of the United States North of the River Ohio came into being. This was the famous Northwest Territory Ordinance which has so many significant local applications including free government, and a prohibition of slavery. In short, a bond of friendship alone was not enough, and the leaders of the American colonies soon realized that a fundamental and enforceable law was inevitable and mandatory.

The Constitution of the United States, adopted September 17, 1787, has been called the greatest work of man in the field of government. The same basic framework of government has worked for 169 years, with but 22 changes, of which 11 occurred before 1800. This means that our fundamental law has required but 11 changes in 155 years, and of these 11, the 21st Amendment repealed the 18th, so in reality there are but nine.

During the War of 1812, which was unpopular in New England, a number of members of the Federalist Party (which was the party who had favored the adoption of the Constitution) sent delegates to a convention at Hartford in 1814, and there proposed a number of constitutional amendments designed to increase state rights at the expense of the federal government. The treaty of peace was signed in time to remove the cause of dissension. However, the arguments used at that time were repeated during the 1850s by Southern states in favor of the right of secession. Curiously enough, the same arguments still crop up in the mouths of certain southern gentlemen who have now adopted a different name to accent the independence of the states from supposedly unwarranted intrusion by the federal government. The current name is "interposition." Interposition is a dialectical approach to a problem which was settled at Appomattox Court House.

As we have said, the basis of the American Constitution is the consent of the governed to cede certain rights to the federal government. The mechanics of its work consist of an amazing system of checks and balances, which makes it quite invulnerable to runaway tampering. It is balanced into three main parts: executive, legislative and judicial, with the power so distributed that liberty should not be in danger. The checks include division of sovereignty between nation and state, frequent popular elections, concurrent jurisdiction of the two houses of Congress, the veto power of the President, the independence of the judiciary, and the confirming power of the senate.

In these days, when the ubiquitous tax collector sends us greetings four times a year for income taxes alone, it seems as though the federal government is completely in charge of our daily lives. So far has this notion gone that many people believe that the federal government is the last resort in every matter, including the courts. Actually, unless there is a so-called federal question in a case, the state courts handle the bulk of the litigation in America, and the court of last resort is the state supreme court. However, it is one of the fundamental rights of our federal constitution that the states must accord every defendant a fair trial. Therefore, it is possible for the judicial system of a state to be so misused that substantial justice is not done. In some of these circumstances, the Supreme Court will intervene.

I am not here to discuss the personalities of our Supreme Court. Judges will differ so long as judges are men instead of gods. But the system of selection of a justice of the United States Supreme Court insures that the man who is eventually appointed must be confirmed by the Senate, and whether or not he appeals to every one of us, that appointee is a very able man and has convinced a very large segment of official America of his worth, and of his value to the judicial system. Human nature is not only the weak link in any system of government- it is also the strongest link. If there is a weak judge, he is surrounded by eight others with equal voice and vote. If there is a strong judge, his strength must be mighty indeed to be recognized above the level of his conferees. Holmes, Brandeis, and the greatest of them all, John Marshall, are names of our greatest men, selected from a body of eminent jurists. These are men who have taken the United States Constitution, applied it to the problems of daily life in a changing world, and have found solutions within its framework. Therein lies the greatness of the system devised by our founding fathers, the constitutional system, and the document itself, the United States Constitution.

The Constitution tells us its purpose in its preamble. "We the people of the United States, in order to form a more prefect Union, establish justice, insure domestic tranquility, provide for the common defense, promote the general Welfare, and secure the blessings of liberty to ourselves and our posterity, do ordain and establish this Constitution for the United States of America."

Although the preamble to the constitution is not in itself an enactment of any law, it describes the nature of the instrument. A constitution is a fundamental organic law for the governance of a society or body. It is important to differentiate between a constitutional provision and an act of Congress. One example is the constitutional provision for an income tax. The sixteenth amendment makes it lawful for the Congress to lay and collect income taxes, without apportionment among the several states. But Congress passes the income tax laws and the laws by which taxes are collected. Without the constitutional provision there could be no income tax. But with it, the wisdom of any tax law is not for the courts to decide. The Supreme Court has often used the following words:

"The wisdom of legislation is a question for Congress. The United States Supreme Court is not concerned with the wisdom of legislation or the need of it. The federal courts cannot render a decision on the political expediency of the statute. If a statute is unfair in its application, the remedy lies with Congress, not with the courts. If laws enacted with good intentions, when put to the test, turn out to be mischievous, absurd or otherwise objectionable the remedy lies with the lawmaking authority and not with the court."

The above quotations are given here to emphasize the difference between a law or statute, and constitutional law. A law may be very silly indeed but still constitutional. The constitution does not give me wisdom - the selection of good men depends upon proper use of the ballot box. But no law, whether silly or wise, may transgress the constitution - and therein lies the great defense against encroachment upon our traditional liberties. For example, the war against crime continues, and the courts are faced with an increasing number of criminal cases. Suppose the Congress should enact a new anti-kidnapping law, and should provide that upon arrest the defendant should immediately be placed upon trial without first being indicted by a grand jury, the purpose of course being to speed up the trial date. This would surely be unconstitutional because the constitution requires both a grand jury indictment and a petit jury conviction before guilt can be established.

The increasing complexities of modern life multiply the problems of lawmakers. The expansion of the philosophy of what some call the "welfare state" creates problems of its own, because the federal government has become involved in making great contributions to many phases of human activity, and is obliged to raise the money and to administer its expenditure. We may add more problems with the passing years. We may and do need more courts to decide more cases. However, this does not mean that we need more Supreme Courts. The Supreme Courts enunciated principles of law, from actual cases, and in theory these principles will be applied by subordinate courts so that although there are more cases, the need for more principles does not increase in the same ratio. The business of the court is already so great that it only hears those cases in which some new principle is involved, or some new law must be interpreted, and even then the case must be of considerable importance. The procedure is for a litigant to file a motion for a writ of certiori. In effect this is a request to the court to hear the case. The court reads the briefs and then the judges meet and determine whether to hear the case. If they do not, the decision of the next lower court is final. If they do, there is a full hearing in open court, followed by a decision, usually with an opinion.

I am not concerned with the pressure of litigation upon the courts, as a matter of fundamental or constitutional law. If the work load becomes too heavy, Congress must appropriate more money for more judges of the district and appellate courts. But I am concerned with a matter of a very different nature, which is fast becoming of extreme importance. I think we will all agree that no longer are we an isolated nation, able to conduct our lives without reference to the world around us. We have had five major wars with foreign powers since the Revolutionary War, all fought on foreign soil. Whether you are a proponent of the One World idea, or not, you are intensely interested in our foreign relations because you have to be.

Agreements between nations are called treaties. Treaties are negotiated by the executive branch of the government, through its State Department, and must then be ratified by the Senate, by a two-thirds vote of members present. When a treaty has been made and ratified, it becomes the supreme law of the land. The constitution provides that "all treaties which shall be made under the authority of the United States shall be the supreme law of the land; and the judges in every state shall be bound thereby, anything in the constitution or laws of any state to the contrary notwithstanding."

At the close of World War II, in another mighty effort to bring about international peace and harmony among the nations of the world, an organization was founded which is called the United Nations Organization. It has been adopted by the United States in the form of a treaty, ratified by the Senate, and has the same status as any other treaty. It is therefore the supreme law of the land and no judge may disregard it. It would seem to follow therefore, that whatever is lawfully done by the United Nations, within the authority of its charter, is binding upon the United States and all other nations who belong to it. Our constitution says that this treaty is the supreme law of the land and therefore our constitution says in effect that the actions of the United Nations, properly authorized, are the supreme law of the United States.

A case arose in California in 1892, over the China Treaty laws of that state with regard to the ownership of land by Asiatics. For years, California had denied ownership of land in California to the many Chinese and other orientals within her borders. However, there was a treaty with China which prevents discrimination in such matters on the ground of race and color. Therefore, a California judge has said that the law of California is unconstitutional as applied to denial of land ownership to a Chinese solely on the ground of his race. We now have a situation where the ratification of a treaty which settled a problem with China now invalidates the legislative action of a state.

So serious are the inherent possibilities of this situation that a very large and determined movement has arisen to enact another amendment to the constitution, which would deny the right of any treaty to affect local laws if the treaty is in conflict with our constitution. The most prominent of these proposed amendments, and the one which is actively under consideration is the so-called Bricker amendment. It would be useful to look at the language of this proposal. It would read:

"Section 1: A provision of a treaty which conflicts with this constitution shall not be of any force and effect.
Section 2: A treaty shall become effective as internal law in the United States only through legislation which would be valid in the absence of treaty.
Section 3: Congress shall have power to regulate all executive and other agreements with any foreign power international organization. All such agreements shall be subject to the limitations imposed on treaties by this article."

A number of prominent and indeed eminent organizations have favored the amendment, including the American Bar Association. Almost an equal number have opposed it. I believe it is significant that amendments to the United States constitution are never taken lightly, and that by the time an amendment is adopted by Congress and then winds its weary way through the 48 states, for ratification by the required three-fourths of them, every possibility has been aired, and the people will have been thoroughly informed. This system is the best insurance against hasty action, and explains in part why the number of surviving amendments to our constitution (aside from the Bill of Rights) is only nine in over a century and a half.

The proponents of the Bricker amendment say:

1st: The three branches of the government cannot be entirely trusted to observe the spirit of the constitution, and therefore it is necessary to impose specific written limitations in foreign affairs matters.
2nd: The need for speed in action upon foreign affairs tends to cause hasty judgments by the federal government, with the possible result that the powers reserved to the states by the constitution can be whittled away, even unwittingly.
3rd: The power of the executive department to make agreements with other nations must be curbed, and Congress must be vested with control over such agreements.

The opponents of the amendment answer, substantially as follows:

1st: In international dealings we must trust someone. The senate has been traditionally cautious in ratifying treaties, and never yet has a treaty signed by the president and ratified by the senate been held unconstitutional.
2nd: The power to make treaties and engage in the handling of foreign affairs must remain with the federal government rather than with the states, and if the amendment is passed, the federal government would be seriously handicapped in its practical ability to function.
3rd: Unless the federal government has a free hand in international dealing, we will become another France, where the legislature is supreme, and where there is no stability of any government, and no assurance that what the department of foreign affairs does will be supported.

This is a very large and serious subject. It is the subject of learned articles by eminent jurists, who are almost equally divided in their opinions. As an example of some of the difficulties, let us consider the following:

Following World War II, an international tribunal was set up by agreement among the victorious nations, to try "war criminals." After conviction of many of these defendants, both at Nuremburg and Tokyo, an appeal was made to the United States Supreme Court, which refused to take jurisdiction on the ground that the tribunal was established by treaty and was not governed by the American constitution. It follows, therefore, that by treaty an international court can be set up which is entirely independent of our bill of rights, and that under certain circumstances our own citizens might be tried by such a tribunal. As a matter of fact the current draft of the International Criminal Court, which is sponsored by the United Nations, contains no requirement for indictment by a grand jury, no adequate protection against forced confessions, and not even the right to trial by jury unless stated in the specific instrument conferring jurisdiction in a particular case. There are many of us who shudder at the results of the Tokyo and Nuremburg trials. I helped to obtain evidence against several Japanese generals and I have a personal feeling on the subject. Personally, I do not believe that General Yamashita had any knowledge of the treatment accorded American prisoners, and it appears to me, from reading the trial records that he was convicted for events for which he was not personally responsible. This is abhorrent to me, although I utterly condemn the Japanese system and especially their treatment of prisoners. But, as a reserve officer, and one who will be called immediately in an emergency, I recognize that my own personal safety from the sentence of a military tribunal depends upon being a winner - not a loser. It is the old story that might makes right. I was surprised and also pleased to hear Senator Taft make the same statement only a year or so before his death.

The issue will become increasingly important when the United Nations shall adopt further legislation on the subjects of human rights and genocide. I believe we shall all be faced with the necessity to make a decision as to the extent to which the United States must surrender its traditional freedoms and liberties to the apparent needs of a world organization. Granted that the striving for world peace will make increasing demands upon us, and that we cannot be a world citizen without assuming responsibility for defining the duties and rights of such citizenship. I am not yet convinced that our traditional liberties and safeguards can be adequately protected under any United Nations enactment until it is subjected to the close and public scrutiny of the people of the United States, with adequate time for debate and searching for the seeds of discord and unAmerican practices. I am not sure that the Bricker amendment is entirely correct as it stands, but I feel the need for equivalent legislation, by constitutional means, as a safeguard to our beloved liberties in this swift moving and tumultuous world.

On Law and Country 113

The Charter of the United Nations is somewhat akin to our old Articles of Confederation, which did not work because they did not have the force of law. Perhaps a One World concept, with a constitution of its own, and provision for enforcing it, may be the ultimate answer. At present, however, none of the world's nations are ready to give up their sovereignty. Another and cataclysmic war might well result in a world state as a matter of absolute necessity for survival. But so long as our relations with others are based upon treaty, which is a contract, and therefore only as good as the integrity of the parties, it behooves us to preserve the freedoms and liberties which we consider fundamental to our lives and the lives of our children. In short, the United States Constitution has given to us what we consider essential to "secure the blessings of liberty to ourselves and our posterity."

RADIO STATION WLEC, SANDUSKY, September 14, 1956

One hundred sixty nine years ago next Monday, the American colonies adopted a framework of government which, with but 22 changes, has guided, protected and promoted us into the most powerful nation on earth and one of the most populous. As a matter of fact, eleven of these changes are known as the Bill of Rights which were adopted shortly after the Constitution itself, before the year 1800. This leaves eleven amendments, but one of these, the 21st, repealed an earlier amendment, the 18th, so actually our system of government has existed for over a century and a half with but nine changes.

There was good reason for enacting our Constitution. The Articles of Confederation had failed to unite the colonies. These articles were little more than a treaty of friendship, anyway, and they lacked the force of law. Of interest to us here in Ohio is the fact that the Ordinance for the government of the Northwest Territory, which included the land where we now live, was adopted by the Confederate Congress in 1787, under the Articles of Confederation. This ordnance provided for free government and prohibited slavery.

The background of any system of government, and the reason for it, are simple. It is the application of its principles which is difficult. Once upon a time, so the Bible state, there was but one man on earth. He needed no law, no constitution. But a short time later, another human being appeared. With her arrival, the population of the world increased 100%, and from that time on, the story of law is the story of the human race. One person, living alone, is concerned only with his own survival and welfare, but as he chooses to live near others, some system must be evolved to reduce the frictions of human intercourse. This system is called law, and it must be enforceable or it is not law. When human beings congregate together, each one must pay a price for the privilege. The price is some part of his former freedom to do as he pleases. Perhaps this price is exacted from him by a tyrant or a dictator who remains all powerful until a stronger power curbs his will. Fortunately for us, our English ancestors decided that the power of the crown should be limited by a set of fundamental and enforceable rules governing life and property, and at Runnymede, in the year 1215, King John was forced to sign that great document of human liberties which we call Magna Carta. The principles then established became the basic governmental philosophy of the English speaking peoples. They evolved into the English constitution, which is unwritten, and into the American Constitution, which is written. In substance, both constitutions are based upon the consent of the governed.

One of the privileges of complete freedom, which America and every one of its states has given to the federal government, is the right to deal with other nations. Only last week the newspapers and radio carried a story concerning negotiations between several northern states and Canada with reference to the St. Lawrence River and the Great Lakes. The Department of State was quoted as objecting to any arrangement which is not made between the federal government of the United States and the Canadian government, which is as it must always be. Somebody has forgotten his history and the Constitution. The degree to which a state has retained the power of government is one of the current national concerns, but I think the problem is pragmatic rather than legal. As early as 1814, some of the New England states, at the Hartford Convention, displeased with the War of 1812, which disrupted their commerce, attempted by a series of resolutions to reaffirm states' rights which they had specifically given up in 1787. There is a modern term which some of our Southern friends are now applying to the subject. It is called "interposition", and it is designed to accent the independence of the states from supposedly unwarranted intrusion by the federal government. The word may be heard again, but practically, interposition is but a dialectical approach to a problem which was resolved 90 years ago.

Our government includes an amazing system of checks and balances, and it was designed that way. It is balanced into three main parts, executive, legislative and judicial, with the power so distributed that liberty should not be in danger. The checks include a division of sovereignty between nation and state, frequent popular election, concurrent jurisdiction of the two houses of Congress, the veto power of the president, the independence of the judiciary and the confirming power of the senate.

It is extremely important to remember that the Constitution is a framework. Within it, Congress makes the laws. A law may be very silly indeed and still be constitutional. The constitution does not give men wisdom; the selection of good lawmakers depends upon proper use of the ballot box. But no law, whether silly or otherwise, may transgress the constitution, and therein lies our great defense against encroachment upon our traditional liberties.

Government, in the enactment of a law, its interpretation, and its application to the problems of mankind, is and must always be the servant of the people. It is the people who must select legislators, judges, and of course the President. If one is inclined to worry over the weaknesses of human nature in government, it is well to remember that it is men and women, democratically selected, who have made our country strong. And it is the Constitution of the United States which at one and the same time circumscribes the actions of the irrational, and permits, indeed motivates the spiritual freedom in which great minds can hold our standards high and make us worthy servants of God.

VETERAN'S DAY
November 11, 1959

When the army decided to reorganize its divisions into the so-called Pentomic type, it selected ten of the twenty-five Reserve divisions for this purpose, six of these ten to be organized at very substantial strength. The 83rd Division, whose headquarters is in Cleveland, Ohio, is one of the six. At the same time, the Army came up with a new idea about unit designations. Some of our Regular Army old time regiments have written the finest pages of American history. But with today's smaller Army, many of these great regiments were only on paper. Therefore, it was decided that the Battle Groups of the modern Pentomic army- which are new and somewhat different from the old infantry regiment- should be designated with the numbers of those grand old regiments. Consequently, in the 83rd Division we now have the 2nd Infantry, the 10th Infantry, the 11th Infantry, the 19th Infantry, the 28th Infantry, complete with their illustrious histories and battle streamers. To man these Battle Groups, the Army selected those elements which, on a geographical basis, could most readily attain a state of training and efficiency, prepared to move into the field in the shortest time. One of the groups thus selected was in this state, and therefore the famous 19th Infantry is a part of the division which I have the honor to command.

Now, lest anyone has the thought that the name and history of these brilliant old regiments have been given to men who are not ready for it, let me correct this impression now. The leadership, in its divisions, Battle Groups, battalions, and even some companies is composed of men who have been in active combat against the enemy in World War II and in Korea and who have continued since then to advance their military knowledge by consistent training, attendance at Service Schools and field duty.

It is common knowledge that the one thing we shall not have, in the event of hostilities, is time. Never again would there be time for Congress to initiate legislation to raise a brand new army from civilian life, clothe it, equip it, send it to training camps, teach it how to cope with modern scientific weapons and equipment. The present philosophy is to provide a small, superbly trained Active Army, and an Army Reserve and a National Guard which is a trained and equipped fighting force, capable of taking the field after the briefest time for last minute preparations. Today, one cannot get into the National Guard or the Reserve unless he has had prior military service or is sent to a training camp immediately upon enlistment. No man can become a non-commissioned officer until he is fully qualified in some military specialty. Nobody is commissioned until he has completed a long period of careful training. No officer can be promoted past first lieutenant until he has demonstrated that his knowledge is equal to a graduate of an army service school of his branch- and we can say that almost all of our officers have attended, are attending, or will attend a branch service school on a resident or non-resident basis. And finally, no officer can be promoted to the highest grades without first having taken the Command and General Staff College course.

    I have taken a bit of time here to talk about some of the basic foundations of the Army Reserve because this is Veterans' Day. A veteran, says Webster's dictionary, is one who has had long experience and practice in any service, industry or art. When the word is used as an adjective, it means "grown old in experience". It actually comes from a Latin word meaning "old". Thus one can be a veteran engineer, veteran miner, veteran lawyer, farmer, carpenter, or mason. It means that one is an old hand at the game, or, more concisely, that he know his business. Certainly the time has come- when every soldier must know his business, for again I say, there will be no time to train him from the ground up. Therefore I am proud to inform you that the Army Reserve and the National Guard are strong, virile components of the Army, and that their members are engaged in serious training so that if they should be needed, no one will doubt that they know their business. In that sense, therefore, they too must be veterans.

Of course, in the popular sense of the term, a veteran is one who has been, or is now, an experienced soldier, sailor, marine or airman. Veterans' Day is the present official name for the day which we formerly used to know as Armistice Day, and that was a day when fighting ceased. It was a day which, for many years was celebrated as the day which ended the war to end all wars. Today it is a day in which we take stock of ourselves and determine whether we have done all that we can do to end all wars. It is the veteran who knows what war is. The veterans who really know are the ones who are not here. It is the veterans who have the basic feeling of what war is, the principal motivation for avoiding another war, and the numerical strength to influence public opinion in the direction in which it must move.

Up in my part of the country*(3), the old time patriotic rallies which used to be held on every Fourth of July are poorly attended. It is just another holiday in which we have fun. I am sorry about this. Despite the heat, the flies, and the sticky candy, I still have a nostalgic yearning for those occasions when everybody as a matter of course turned out and took off their hats when the flag passed by. By some insidious process, in some indefinable way, it brought us together in a common cause- the cause of Americanism. Today, we rather cringe at being called patriots. It is not a popular word. But would you cringe at being likened to a man who won a Medal of Honor? Are you not proud that the typical American service man conducted himself with distinction? What would be your reaction if a foreigner were to tell you that the American soldier is no good? And yet I have heard so many foolish statements, engendered by fuzzy thinking, that I have wondered about it. I suspect that this is the era of "broad-mindedness".

It is a fine thing to be broad-minded, but there is such a thing as being too broad-minded. In morals, we can be so indulgent of the sins of others that somewhere along the line we lose our own moral perspective. We can be so broad-minded about religion that we have none of our own.

What with the speed of activities all around us, with the newspaper, radio and television giving us the news as soon as it happens, we are kept pretty well off balance. We do not have time to digest yesterday's news because we are so busy with today's. Time was when father read the paper at home, and the family was in the same room. Father was the oracle, and when he pronounced his opinion upon some international event, the impression on the children was deep and abiding. Furthermore, it was his own opinion. Where he read of a local scandal and mother pursed her lips and said what she thought, there was no doubt in anyone's mind that some things are right and some things are wrong. The *words* were used: *right* and *wrong*. Today, such is the tempo of living, so great is the impression made by the scientific approach to every aspect of life, social, political, mechanical, moral, that we are overwhelmed by the very abundance of information- and we are in danger of using the canned opinions of others instead of thinking for ourselves, in those areas where our opinions are just as valid as the other fellow's.

The opinion of the military veteran is an educated opinion. Who is this veteran of our wars- the G.I.? Well, when he entered the service he was a farm boy, a college student, a clerk. Perhaps he came from a big city where life is supposed to be a little easier. He became physically and mentally an alert, intelligent and effective fighting man. He fought on foreign soil, and the reasons for fighting there were very complicated and just a little too involved for him to understand completely. He probably was a draftee, and he didn't like the draft but he knew it was necessary. His gripes and beefs about the military service were loud and long but he was a good solider. He comes from a free country. If you told him he was a great patriot he would laugh at you, but on the record he demonstrated the deepest kind of patriotism and courage. He disliked the regimented discipline which must be a component of every military service, but he accepted it because it too was necessary. His parents or ancestors, or even he himself, may have been born in a foreign country, but it was only our enemies who made the mistake of believing that he was not an American all the way. *Remember* this: he has never been licked.

Let me repeat: the opinion of the veteran is an educated opinion. Today, we find ourselves in a period of technological development. We are surrounded by evidence of exotic weapons. And yet the veteran knows, by experience, intuitively, that the historic role of the ground combat soldier has never changed and that it never will. Whether this soldier arrives by way of the ground, the sea, or through the air, in the last analysis, he must seize and hold the ground. The ultimate weapon is man. As General Bruce Clark says: "The ground soldier is not and never will be replaced by anything that fissions, flies or floats".

For the past year or two we have been talking a good deal about the size of the armed forces. The discussions are caused by the need to combat unnecessary governmental expenditures on the one hand, and the need to protect ourselves on the other hand. Today we have an Active Army of 800,000, and Army Active Reserve of 300,000, and an Army National Guard of 400,000. There are those who think we should cut down the size of the whole army, regular and reserve, and there are other who honestly believe that the present strength is far too little. I am not here today to fight for a *large* army or navy or air force or Marine Corps. But I could not stand before you in good conscience if I did not tell you that I will fight with anyone, anywhere, anytime, who even so much as intimates that the United States should not have the *best* army, the *best* navy, the *best* air force, and the *best* Marines in the world. It is quality that counts. The quality of an army derives primarily from the men who are in it, and then from their leadership, training, and equipment. Therefore, every veteran and every citizen will agree, I am sure, that while he is engaged in civilian occupation, he will sleep soundly at night only if he knows that the protection of his family and home is entrusted to the kind of army on which he can rely.

Even though the veteran reserves his well earned right to criticize, nevertheless, he has an instinctive feeling that what he sees in the present army is either good or it is bad. He can help make it good and keep it good by speaking out boldly and often. For example:

1st. The size of the Army, the Army Reserve and the National Guard is critical. When he hears talk of reducing it, he should bore in and ask why- and he should insist upon good answers.

2nd. Development of new weapons is as important today as it was when the cross-bow replaced the spear, or when gunpowder replaced the sword. He should insist that no country in the world be armed with better weapons than we have.

3rd. The uniformed soldier, sailor, marine or airman is just an ordinary fellow like you and me, but his uniform signifies that he knows how to do a job when the country needs to have it done. Joke and kid with the man, if you know him, but don't sell him short, and don't undercut his uniform.

4th. Support the National Guardsman and the Reservist in our country. He and his buddies will be your sword and your shield if the need arises.

Another change is taking place in the Army- in fact, it has taken place. It is a concept called "ONE ARMY". The principal is, that no longer do we have a Regular Army, a National Guard or an Army Reserve. What we have is one army, composed first of those who spend full time on the job (the active army); second, the active reservists who spend a great deal of time with their National Guard or Reserve units; and third, the inactive reserve, which is a great reservoir of manpower with military training which can be fully trained in a relatively short time. But the Active Army, the Active Reserve and the National Guard are part of one army right now. They take the same training, use the same weapons and training camps, and work out of the same rule books. They are inspected by the same inspectors and graded by the same standards. They wear the same uniform, and you can't tell the difference between them. What we are doing is molding an American soldier-the finest soldier in the world.

I have had the great privilege of serving from time to time with other services. Although I have talked here about the Army, because I am in the Army, nevertheless, I know that the Navy, the Marine Corps and the Air Force are following the same principles as the Army. I was aboard a Navy destroyer bound for Guadalcanal, a Navy transport bound for Bougainville, I have flown over the South Pacific in a Navy bomber, I served with my Army battalion in the First Marine Amphibious Corps at Bougainville, and I have participated in many a venture with the Army Air Corps, which is now the Air Force. I have served as a reservist, as a National Guardsman, and as a member of the Army of the United States. It is therefore with some background of experience that I personally vouch for the high motivation, dedicated effort, and practical effectiveness of the Navy, the Marine Corps and the Air Force, including their Reserve Components. I have been an artilleryman, a doughfoot in combat with the infantry, a staff officer, and a commander. I hope you will excuse these personal references. All I am doing is telling you that I am a *veteran*, and that as a veteran, I have watched all the arms and all the services of the United States Armed Forces and I am proud as I can be, of all of them. This is Veterans' Day, a day when veterans of past wars, and their families and friends are entitled to know what is being done today to keep faith with them.

Well, I can tell you that service in the armed forces today is on the most stimulating level it has ever attained. The impact of modern science, the troubles and uncertainties of the Free World, threatened by the menace of Communism, and above all, the determination of the solider to be good at his job- all of these things have combined to produce Armed Forces that will respond to the will of the people. If you want them to be good, and if you support them, they can and they will be good. And if the great host of veterans in this country, who far outnumber any other category of citizen, *really want it*, our Armed Forces will not only be good, but will be better than any enemy they would ever face. As veterans, let us remember that in a major conflict there is no prize for second place. The only prize is for the winner, and the prize is freedom and life itself.

There is a moral in all this. The United States is no nearer to a military dictatorship than it was in the 1920s, when we let our guard down completely. This country is run by civilians. Every one of the Armed Service is headed by a civilian who was approved by the Senate. Every general, every admiral (whether regular or reserve) was promoted only after the Senate confirmed his nomination. Every piece of military equipment, down to the last shoe string was purchased with funds appropriated by Congress. Every Congressman and every Senator was elected by the people. Our military system is completely under the control of the people of these United States, and that is the way, thank God, it should be. In these days of complicated fast moving events, when we are surrounded by many seemingly unsolvable problems, the real and present danger is that the citizenry will forget or neglect to express their opinions on those matters on which their opinions are valuable. The opinion of the veteran is an informed opinion. It is not necessary that he make a detailed decision, that is the job of his servants, the trained military experts. But it *is* his job, and a vital one, to see to it that the safety of our country has top priority, and that no congestion of legislative business shall ever permit any other subject to have precedence. I am certain that the members of the Congress will welcome this kind of support, for they are greatly pressed with problems, and yet are most emphatically desirous of accepting in full measure the responsibility for national security that is placed upon them. It is well to recall again and again that we can be so broad-minded and tolerant of the complexities of government that we can fail to stand up boldly and assert the basic premise, that the safety of our people must come first. The lesson taught to us by the veteran, who is no longer here, is that today's veteran- the trained soldier- is the man who by his very existence may keep tomorrow's veteran off the battlefield, and our country out of war.

CITIZENSHIP AND THE COLD WAR
Sandusky 1960

Many years ago a group of women met periodically for literary purposes. The subjects presented were the biographies of authors or they were book reviews. In any event, the subject matter was important. One day the subject was "The Great Religions of the World," and the matter was concluded in one hour. This is about the way one approaches the subject of the Constitution and National Defense, except that I shall not impose upon you for an hour.

It is important to summarize the arguments on the Connally Amendment. Here they are:

1. Foundation: The World Court is called the International Court of Justice. It was created by the charter of the United Nations to decide the following matters:
"All cases which the parties refer to it and all matters especially provided for the Charter of the United Nations or in treaties and conventions in force."

2. Although all members of the United Nations subscribed to its charter, yet submission to the jurisdiction of the World Court was not compulsory, and all member nations were given the opportunity to file an acceptance of the court's compulsory jurisdiction if they desired it. The so-called Connally amendment arose out of the discussions in the Senate with regard to whether or not the United States would accede to compulsory juris-

diction of the World Court, for the United States. Article two of the U.N. Charter specifically prohibits the court from exercising jurisdiction over matters which are essentially within the domestic jurisdiction of any state. When the Senate acted on the matter, it specifically said that its declaration of accepting compulsory jurisdiction should not apply to "disputes with regard to matters which are essentially within the domestic jurisdiction of the United States of America." At this point, the Senate said what the charter had already said, and therefore there were no points of difference. But the senate then added the following words: "as determined by the United States of America."

There is no objection to the first words, but the insertion of the latter makes the United States the only judge of whether or not in a given case it will permit the court to have jurisdiction. This is the problem. As soon as we inserted these words, eight other nations copied the idea, namely: England, France, India, Mexico, Pakistan, Liberia, Sudan, and the Union of South Africa. Shortly thereafter came the news that Russia had the atomic bomb, the H-bomb, satellites and the intercontinental ballistic missile, and it became clearly apparent that unless this was the preferred method of settling disputes, we had better have a court.

Accordingly, England, India and France dropped the self-judging clause from the acceptance, and they now have acceded full compulsory jurisdiction of the World Court.

Thirty-three other nations have accepted without the reservation. All the leading countries of the world have so accepted except the United States and Russia. Russia has not accepted jurisdiction at all. But since the United States has accepted only on the condition that she approves jurisdiction as to each dispute, it follows that the positions of the United States and Russia are about the same. This stems from a curious incident.

Norway had issued gold bonds in France, then went off the gold standard. France on behalf of her investors, commenced an action in the World Court for adjudication of the alleged repudiation of the terms of payment. But France had the self-judging clause in its acceptance of the court's jurisdiction, so Norway said that if France reserved its own judgment in such matters, certainly the option was reciprocal, and Norway declared that whether or not she was on the gold standard was a domestic matter and not within the jurisdiction of the court. The court agreed, and threw out France's case. It is the law, therefore, that if a nation has agreed to the court's jurisdiction only on the condition that she and she alone may decide whether the jurisdiction extends to the matter in dispute, reciprocal rights exist in the other party, and the court cannot decide at all. Immediately, France withdrew her conditional acceptance. So did England. In fact, there are only five small nations who stand with Russia and the United States.

As an illustration, if we were to sue Panama in the world court, to enforce a treaty provision about the Panama Canal, Panama could say that it was a domestic matter and the court would throw out the case. In other words, we have nullified our use of the court.

The elimination of the Connally amendment has been urged by: President Eisenhower, President Truman; Vice President Nixon; Senator Kennedy; Secretaries of State Dulles, Herter and Acheson; Attorney General Rogers; Senators Fulbright and Symington and many others.

The United States has filed seven complaints with the world court for damages for attacks upon our airplanes. Six of them have been thrown out by the Soviet Union, Czechoslovakia, Bulgaria, and Hungary who refused to consent to the court's jurisdiction. The Communists distrust the world court. Unfortunately, so does the U.S. In this state of affairs, there is no judicial tribunal to decide any international issue concerning the U.S. or the Communist countries.

There are many more arguments for repeal of the Connally amendment. There are many arguments for its retention. Among these, the most persuasive is that the judges of the world court include jurists from Communist countries and that in the event of a close vote, the power of decision would lie in the hands of judges whose motives and personal integrity are suspect. There are fifteen judges, and the term is nine years. Terms of five judges expire every three years. It would take nine years to change the entire personnel of the court. However, we have reserved the right to withdraw from the court upon six months' notice. Therefore, if the complexion of the court should change in a manner deemed injurious to the U.S., we could withdraw before the change of court personnel would become significant.

I think it is a true statement, however, that the judges, even the Communist judges, have so far evidenced a very clear intention to respect domestic rights of sovereign nations, and to veer away from placing a dispute in the international law category unless it belongs there.

The actual objection of sincere opponents of compulsory jurisdiction is fear of involvement of the United States in foreign affairs. There is a complete lack of trust in the Communist ethic. With this I agree. But let us remember that we are not talking about a world state- the United Nations of the World, with a president, a legislature, a court, and compulsory enforcement machinery. I do not believe the world has approached the point where we can consider world government. All we can do now is to take such steps as will start the minds of all working in the direction of a rule of law rather than a rule of force. We know in this country, perhaps better than do others, that a partnership of sovereign states will not work. Our experience under the Articles of Confederation is known to all of us. It was the lack of trust in each other that led to its dissolution, and the substitution of our present form of government under the Constitution. But even this form of government was distrusted by many. Even after the Constitution was ratified, it became necessary to reassure everybody by the adoption of the Bill of Rights, or the first ten amendments.

Today, we are faced with the possibility of annihilation by military force. I use the word possibility deliberately, for I do not believe we are about to experience a world conflict of arms. In military circles, when we talk about the enemy, we do not come right out and say what he will do. What we say is that he has certain capabilities. We are a world of people, and are subject to human weaknesses. We know that if a sovereign nation has the capability of launching a successful attack, then it is our responsibility to prepare to meet it so that if it should occur, it will not be successful.

The military intelligence expert does not say what the enemy *will* do, but what he *can* do. None of us know what the Communist countries *will* do, but we know what they *can* do. And we have adopted policies aimed at containing his capabilities. Every time a new weapon has been invented, somebody has invented a specific defense against it. The weapon comes first, then the defense. The interval between the two is vital. That is why we must at all times have the best military and scientific minds continually at work, developing every possibility so that never shall we be only second best.

But there also comes a time when the magnitude of the weapons system out-distances the earth we live on. When a canon ball was eight inches in diameter, we figured a way to avoid standing on the target. We moved sideways, or strengthened the fort. When an artillery shell was developed that covered an area of 100 yards, the problem was more difficult but was solved. But when a hydrogen bomb has the capability of extinguishing everything under it over an area five miles square, with radiation and blast effects over a still greater area, and worst of all, with fall-out capabilities covering a whole state, and when we multiply the effect of single bomb by the number of bombs which might be loosed, we must face up to the proposition that we must either come up with a complete defense, or we must find a way to stop the holocaust. As sensible human beings, the rule of law is the goal.

Just this week, a Nike Hercules missile was sent up to destroy another Nike Hercules missile. The combined speed of the two was about seven times the speed of sound. The defensive missile was successful. It searched out and found the other one, in flight, and destroyed it. Perhaps we can develop defensive mechanisms which will stop every form of offensive missiles. But as missiles get bigger, and faster, and better, and go higher into the air, the problem becomes more difficult. This is the present race of armament.

You recall, of course, that Teddy Roosevelt said "Speak softly and carry a big stick." We must keep the big stick. Unfortunately, the new weapons at the disposal of any prosperous nation are such that it is nothing short of catastrophic to have inferior equipment. It is the age old fact that a good big man is better than a good little man. That is the way it is. But the search for new and more efficient weapons brings with it new problems. For example let us consider the matter of air space.

Our original idea of property rights was based upon our knowledge of what we could do with it. We used to say that when a man bought land, he owned it clear to the sky, and down to the center of the earth. At first he could not get into the sky, and so it did no harm for a land owner to lie on his back and survey the majesty of his upper domain. But he did learn to dig down under the ground, and eventually he weakened the earth around his coal mine so that his neighbor's earth caved in and his house fell down. An early English court decided that even if a man did own his ground down to the center of the earth, there was a practical limit to what he could do with it, and if he hurt his neighbor, he was liable.

And now we can occupy the space above the ground, and we know that it has long been the law that an airplane, traveling high over the earth across our homes, is not trespassing. However, we regulate such travel, as a matter of government for the benefit of all, and we have decided that if an airplane unnecessarily flies so close to the earth as to cause damage on the ground, the operator of the plane is liable for it.

But where does sovereignty terminate? The earth is round. Is our boundary determined by a line drawn from the center of the earth to the edge of our property- and then up? How high? 100,000 feet? If a foreign plane flies over the United States at an altitude of 100,000 feet, is it trespassing? I think the answer is yes. But how about an object sent into orbit, that flies over Sandusky two or three times a night hundreds and perhaps thousands of miles up? Is it trespassing? We may say that it is not, but suppose it contained wonderful new photographic equipment and made pictures of the ground beneath in such fine detail that enlargements could be made? And suppose the camera was launched by the Soviet Republic? Or conversely, by us, and it mapped the world, including Russia. Mr. Powers, in the U-2, was called a spy. How about Mr. John Doe or Ivan Ivanovitch, three hundred miles aloft?

We have put objects high into space and then released the nose capsule, calculated where it would land, and then landed it there, by pressing the right button. We even fished one of the nose capsules out of the air before it landed. In a short time we shall be able to launch a nose capsule to land where we choose. We could load it with a nuclear weapon. We shall have the capability of doing so, very soon. So will the Red countries.

I think that there is no doubt at all that the capability for complete destruction of any section of the earth now exists, and that within a very short time we shall have so improved our techniques that accuracy can be obtained, within very narrow limits. I believe that our ability to retaliate against an enemy is now sufficient to constitute a positive deterrent to an all-out nuclear war. I believe that this power of retaliation is the only force which can and which will restrain the Communists from pursuing a policy of annihilation of the people of the United States. I believe that we must *never* have a weapons system secondary to that of another power. I do *not* believe that the resultant armament race will bankrupt us all, and that we shall soon be divided into two armed camps. I believe that the now existing weapons systems, for long destruction, has proceeded far enough so that no one, even with a better system, can escape retaliation in the form of utter destruction. It is possible, although highly improbable, to develop a weapons system which is so accurate that it could knock out every missile launching site located on the ground, and that therefore, the power which first launches these weapons could prevent return fire from the ground. But to accomplish this result, it would be necessary to know accurately the location of each site. This would not include the submarine, which is now capable of launching the Polaris missile, from a submerged position. In other words, the submarine is a moving launching site, hidden from view, responsive to radio orders from its headquarters, and capable of delivering the retaliatory fire power which is feared by all. That is why I say that *already* we have reached the point where the means of retaliation now exist, on a practical level, so that no nation on earth could launch a nuclear attack without being destroyed, itself, in turn.

If this is true, then what may we expect from our Communist neighbors? Well, on this point I have a positive attitude. I believe that the gradual infiltration of Communist doctrine into the Western world is proceeding at so alarming a pace that already South America is in jeopardy of capitulation. I fully believe that Castro will suffer serious reverses, and that his regime will never succeed. I rather expect to read almost any day, that he has been assassinated. But that is not the point. He has permitted so many Soviet and Chinese Reds to enter Cuba, and they have become so firmly entrenched in the minds of the Cuban people, that Cuba is now and will continue to be a Communist country, and the Caribbean will be a Russian lake; I think that you can count on it, within five years. I do not think that there is any country in either South or Central America which can withstand Communist infiltration. I believe that we shall be surrounded.

Do you know that Red propaganda in South American already uses forty hours of radio time per week? Do you know that Communist Chinese, in person, are coming to Cuba and to South America every week? If you were to visit the right places in South America, you would find large numbers of Chinese, well financed, conducting large scale business operations? Do you know that this is a Communist front, and that incitement to riot, undermining of security, and eventual suppression of liberty is their ultimate goal?

Do you actually believe that when South Americans spit on our Vice President, and when Japanese students rioted to prevent the visit of President Eisenhower, that these were simple manifestations of displeasure? And how did their governments handle the situation? In South America, with troops. The police scarcely dared to interfere. In Japan, by calling off the visit. The government was not capable of restraining the mobs.

Let us take a few moments to look at the box score:

1. Soviet Georgia. Independence proclaimed in 1920, invaded by Stalin in 1921.
2. The Ukraine. Treaty of Alliance in 1920. Forcibly annexed in 1922.
3. Poland. Non-aggression pact in 1932. Partitioned in 1939.
4. Estonia. Mutual Assistance Treaty 1939. Forcibly annexed 1940.
5. Latvia. Mutual Assistance Treaty 1939. Forcibly annexed 1940.
6. Lithuania. Mutual Assistance Treaty 1939. Forcibly annexed 1940.
7. Czechoslovakia. Mutual Assistance Treaty 1943. Communist Party took over in 1940.
8. Hungary. Peace Treaty 1947. Communist Party and Soviet troops took over in 1949.
9. Rumania. Peace Treaty 1947. Communist Party and Soviet troops took over in 1948.

10. Bulgaria. Peace Treaty 1947. Communist Party and Soviet troops took over in 1948.

ACTS OF WAR:
1. Indonesian War 1945-1947
2. Chinese Civil War 1945-1949
3. Malayan War 1945-1954
4. Philippine Civil War 1945-1948
5. Indochina War 1945-1954
6. Greek Guerrilla War 1945-1949
7. Kashmir Conflict 1947-1949*
8. Arab-Israel War 1948-1949*
9. Korean War 1950-1953
10. Guatemalan Revolt 1954
11. Argentine Revolution 1955*
12. Algerian War 1954 ----
13. Cyprus War 1955-1959*
14. Sinai Campaign*
15. British-Suez Campaign 1956*
16. Hungarian Suppression 1956
17. Muscat and Oman Operations 1957*
18. Indonesian Civil War 1958 ----
19. Lebanon and Jordan Operations 1958*
20. Formosa Strait Conflict 1958
21. Cuban Civil War 1958-1959
22. Tibetan Revolt 1958-1959
23. Laotian Conflict 1960
24. The Congo 1960

Of the above named incidents, the first eight were pulled into the Soviet Empire. Of the remaining 24 incidents, all but eight (the ones with the asterisk) were fomented by Communists, who have supplied arms and economic aid.

And now, in the light of a Communist intention to take over the earth, what is the posture of our Armed Forces? What is the structure that our military heads should provide for our security?

Well, first of all, we must retain the power of massive retaliation, by nuclear weapon, with adequate delivery means by plane and missile. And these techniques must be the best on earth. Second, we must have magnificently trained armed forces, divided into tactical groups, and supplied with the means of air delivery to any spot on earth. Under the Soviet system of encirclement, not only is there propaganda and infiltration, there is also active conflict, on a small scale, at several points on the earth's surface, each of which ends in a Soviet dominated area. The only possible way to stop this type of encirclement is by occupying the ground with well trained troops, possessed of the most efficient weapons and skillfully led. We have seen with dismay, how the United Nations troops have been thwarted in the Congo, by a directive which prevents them from using their weapons. And while U.N. troops have been embarrassed at their ineffectiveness, all the Communist countries' delegations at the United Nations have actively urged the withdrawal of these troops so that Russian "so-called aid" can become effective and so that Russia can take over the Congo. But suppose a similar situation at Guantanamo Bay, in Cuba. There, it will be the United States. In Germany, where we have ground forces, it would be the United States. In Korea, were we keep troops, it would be the United States, as it was before.

The modern United States Army, small as it is, is the best we have ever had. The Regular Establishment, at least in the Strategic Striking Force, is highly trained, and consists of men with an alertness, soldierly bearing, and capability that is outstanding. We also have a well trained Reserve of 300,000 and a National Guard of 400,000. The contrast between these men and the Reserve and Guard of 1939 is fantastic. And yet there are those in government who would reduce the size of our little army and of our Reserve forces, and put all our security into the Air Force.

The problem is not simple. We can spend so much on our over-all military preparedness that we could play right into Communist hands by weakening ourselves economically, and becoming easier prey to propaganda, infiltration and rotting away from within. But these are scare words, and are usually uttered by men who are making a hard sell but do not know the facts. Actually, the Soviet Union is spending more money, both in actual rubles, and percentage-wise to its national budget, upon its military system, than we are. In terms of standards of living, Russia is willing to accept an austerity program in order to conquer the world, and that she intends to do. Much that she spends is upon her missionary system.

If every dollar that every church in the Western World has ever spent to send missionaries to convert the heathen were added up, that sum would not support the missionary activity of the Union of Soviet Socialist Republics for the year 1960. When the Russian missionaries go to the Congo, they speak the proper African dialect, which they have been learning for some years, in anticipation of this activity. Russian missionaries in South America speak Spanish or Portuguese. They know the Arabic dialects. In the far east, in Laos, in Indonesia, in Korea, and Japan the missionaries from Communist countries speak the local language fluently. Their converts are the people in the villages, with whom they associate on intimate terms. To paraphrase Caesar, all the world is divided into *two* parts, and one of them is getting bigger at the expense of the other.

Now what can we do about it? I believe that the approach is from two directions. First, whatever we do, we must be strong, for the Communist despises a weakling and respects strength. Second, we must use the best minds of our best statesmen to come closer and closer to a realization that sovereign rights of individual nations must become integrated into participation in a worldwide partnership. We are not ready for world government, but we must survive. The powers of good have always been capable of matching the powers of evil, but today the practical application of righteous thinking and living spells the difference between life and death. I have five grandchildren, and not one of them ever heard of Communism. It is not the purpose of my life to sell them into bondage.

Let me close with the words of General Omar Bradley: "The state is an invention of men. It has neither intellect, nor conscience, no morals. It is an inanimate machine. And where the machine is master of the man it is simply fueled by his obedience, his fatigue and his terror."

A democracy such as ours cannot be defeated in this struggle; it can only lose by default.

It can only lose if our people deny through indifference and neglect their personal responsibilities for its security and growth.

Our danger lies not so much in a fifth column whose enmity is avowed. It lies in a first column of well meaning American citizens who are one hundred per cent Americans in their daily protestations, and ten percent citizens in their routine of neglect.

A TOAST TO DANIEL D. WHITE
At Sandusky Kiwanis Club On the Occasion of His 100th Birthday Tuesday, May 16, 1961

We are here today to honor a member of this club who has held the respect and esteem of this entire community longer than any other living person. In several respects, this day is unique. Before his 100th birthday, Dan White was only 99 years old, and thereafter never again will he be so young. Here is a man, more than half of whose life has been untouched by the income tax, and two-thirds of it before Social Security was even thought of.

The magic in today's meeting is found in the number 100, but it is also found in the character of our friend Dan White. Merely to *exist* for 100 years is remarkable, but that came about because God willed it so. To *live* for 100 years is a different matter, for there the man himself must make choices. Here we have a man who has lived a full and active life, who has been a producer instead of a consumer, and who has stood in the sight of God and his neighbors for 100 years of *responsible* living.

As we prepare to seat ourselves at the luncheon table, and to enjoy the great privilege of his companionship, let us drink a toast to our honored guest, our friend, our fellow Kiwanian, this wonderful man and centenarian: DANIEL D. WHITE.

TRIBUTE TO A WAR OF 1812 HERO
May, 1961

It is with great pleasure that I join you today as a representative of the United States Army, in this rededication exercise, to pay tribute to an old soldier. On this day as on other great occasions throughout the country, we pause from our business, social and personal activities to look backward to the foundations of our nation. In doing so we are often surprised to find that we live in a world of people; that all the events of our history are recorded in terms of the men and women who produced these events. Even the great catastrophes of nature, earthquakes, storms, fire and flood are considered in relation to their effects on people and, above all, how people reacted to them.

In the last few years have occurred the most astonishing revelations of the forces of nature. Only this past week we have witnessed the dramatic penetration of outer space by a member of our Armed Forces. When we look at pictures and at televised records of this dramatic event, we see an Air Force officer propelled into space as the result of the combined efforts of all sorts of men who together constitute the great team which is required to harness the infinite forces of nature. It has been well demonstrated that men have learned more about the composition of matter and nature's laws in the past twenty years than in the entire period of the world's history. To the uninformed in such matters, the men who reveal these secrets and utilize this new knowledge are geniuses, and so they may be, but it has also been said that genius is the infinite capacity for detail, patience, and hard work. The Air Force officer, in his space capsule, was launched with the concurrence of effort of every resource for which there was need, and, at the conclusion of his journey, the capsule was sighted over eighty miles in the air on the radar of a navy carrier positioned to recover him. Then the capsule was retrieved by an ordinary sailor in a boat, the same kind of sailors who have manned boats since the earliest days of recorded time.

Every branch of the Armed Forces has been converted into a composite organization, segments of which are capable of commanding the air, the ground, the surface of the sea and the ocean's depths. The modern infantry platoon has the mobility and the weapons with which to command as much ground space as formerly required a regiment. Each man is specially trained, and, after such training, he is relied on by his buddies to do his job. Soldiers are positioned at great distances from each other. Each man must be staunch, for if he gives ground, the vacant interval cannot be quickly filled, and the loss may be irretrievable. Again, the radar on ground, sea, or in the air may detect objects at tremendous distances.

The information it gathers is more than could be learned by whole squadrons of cavalry, or fleets of ships, or hundreds of civil war balloons, but what does the radar do? It reveals on a screen spots of light, which, properly interpreted, indicate the nature and movement of objects. But they are only spots of light until a *man* looks at them, and interprets them, and translates his interpretation into words, and communicates these facts to others quickly enough to trigger decisions and resulting action. And here we are again- back to a man.

It is said that Colonel McPherson, whom we honor today, acted as a spy for General Clark and for General Hull.*(4) It takes little imagination to conjure up in our mind's eye the risks he took to penetrate enemy lines, or to travel in uncleared forests among Indians and hostile inhabitants. What he did, and what the soldiers and sailors of his day did, in the environment in which they moved, gave us our nation. Their courage, patriotism, and skill were the basic ingredients of success, and the courage, patriotism and skill of every man in our Armed Forces today are the basic ingredients of our security. It is man who rules the earth- not things.

As we consider the mobility of character which is the essential ingredient of our nation's heroes, we should be profoundly moved when we know that our nation cannot survive without heroes. Indeed, the world cannot survive without heroes. Tomorrow's heroes are the sons and brothers and friends of all of us present here today, the men who are serving in our Armed Forces. We here, and all the members of the Armed Forces today and tomorrow, and those who served us since the time of the Revolution, are united in a great brotherhood, the loss of any one of whom diminishes us. As John Donne said: "Any man's death diminishes me, because I am involved in mankind, and therefore never send to know for whom the bell tolls; it tolls for thee."

This is a great brotherhood, and we are all part of it, and responsible for it. The rededication exercises here today will impress indelibly on our consciousness this feeling of respect and kinship with all the members of the Armed Forces of the United States who have preceded us, who are here today, and who will guard our nation in the future. God grant that we shall keep the faith.

BOY SCOUT OCCASION
"Using Your Time"
1966

When Mr. Roesch called me some days ago and invited me to be with you tonight, I asked him what I should talk about. I meant, of course, what should be the subject matter, but his answer was that I should talk about 10 or 15 minutes. After I hung up the telephone, it occurred to me that unknowingly, he had presented me with an excellent subject. Ten or 15 minutes is therefore not only the time I shall consume, but also, it is the subject. The more I thought about it, the more I realized the amazing importance of all the 10 minute and 15 minute intervals that have been lost by me and I do not intend to be critical when I suggest that they may be lost by you, too.

The proper use of time is not only important- it is the very essence of our passage through this world, for we shall never have the day to live over again- or even 10 minutes. Nothing is as irretrievable as time.

In the business world, everything done takes time. Time equals money, and the business world revolves about money. Industrial production is measured by the number of acceptable products that come off the machines in a given time. To the farmer, the value of a cow is the quantity of milk it gives in twenty-four hours, and a hen's value is measured by the number of eggs she lays within the brief span of her egg-laying life. A journalist for a newspaper has a deadline to make, and if he omits some of the facts or misses his deadline, his stature as a journalist is not improved. It is often said the only things a professional man has to sell are his time and his advice. In banking circles within the great metropolitan areas, the handling of checks and deposits has reached so great a volume that all the massive bookkeeping machines that can be purchased are not sufficient, and so many banks have purchased computers. I read the other day that the computer used by a great New York bank blew a fuse or had a short circuit or had some internal malady, with the result that over one billion dollars of figures piled up in the bank, and the telephones were swamped by customers demanding their clearances.

Literature is filled with allusions to time and its uses. For example, "time flies;" "time and tide wait for no man." Shakespeare says: "One man in his time plays many parts," or as The Reverend Mr. Keble said: "Till time and sin together cease."

Time has many meanings.

1) It is the interval between two events.
2) It is an exact moment in the calendar.
3) It means "now," as for example, now is the time for all good men to come to the aid of the party.
4) It means the pay check, as when a man says to the cashier "I want my time" or my "overtime."
5) It is a measure or cadence in music or marching. A waltz is written in three part time. I could go on. We speak of dinner time, bed time, summertime, daytime, night time. And so it goes.

In all of these allusions to time, we have considered only what time means affirmatively. I think there is another meaning. What can be said of the interval between two events when nothing happens? That, too is the passage of time. In that period our brains and bodies have aged, some of the old cells have died and new cells have arrived. If we are growing, we continue to grow, even if we do absolutely nothing. If we are old we wear out a little more. But I am not really concerned about Boy Scouts doing nothing. As I look about me, it seems that every boy who is old enough to be a Scout has a continuous program of something doing most of the time. Between school, home chores, Scout activities and meeting, music lessons, team practice, club duties, church and Sunday School, eating, sleeping and playing, the problem really is not *whether* you are doing something, but *what* you are doing. If you sit down and analyze everything you did you will find that you probably had a busy day. How busy? Let me suggest that you try a professional approach to a 24 hour period now and then, and every few minutes write down what you have been doing so that you have a really accurate record. Then, for the first time, you will probably find that every day is filled with 10 and 15 minute periods for which you cannot account. You may find a dozen such periods or even more. Twelve times ten minutes is two hours. If you get up at seven and go to bed at nine or ten, you will have had 14 or 15 hours in your day, but 2 hours is about *one-seventh* of the whole day. One seventh of a year is more than seven weeks.

My purpose is not to suggest what you should do with most of your time. I just want to talk about some of the things that you can do in 10 or 15 minutes, now and then.

I once knew the Headmaster of a school who kept a copy of the Bible in his bathroom. I found this out because he knew more about the Bible than anyone I ever encountered and I asked him how he knew so much. He said that it took him fifteen minutes to shave, so he always opened the Bible on a table beside the wash-stand and reads a few verses each morning. When I knew him he was about 60 years old, he had been shaving for over 40 years, and I calculated that he could have read the Bible for 3,640 hours just while shaving. His familiarity with the Bible was apparent and he never had to grope through his memory. If it was important enough to be remembered, he recalled it.

The other day I had a letter from someone in Vietnam. During the troop movement, somehow his copy of the Bible he had acquired upon graduation from West Point had been lost. The chaplain loaned him a copy of the Revised Standard Edition, but eventually his wife sent him the King James edition which he liked. He said that he never before realized how much satisfaction there was in reading the Bible until he had been without one for some weeks, and then had the opportunity to turn on his flashlight in his pup tent and read the familiar words. Do you read your Bible, or do you let someone else read it to you on Sunday? How about using some of those 15 minute periods?

The newspapers and magazines are filled with news originating out of Vietnam, but I am amazed at some of the comments I hear on the streets about this situation, or even about Vietnam. What are the differences between the people who live in North Vietnam and in South Vietnam? What are the differences between the geographical characteristic of the two countries? Why are there two countries anyway, and when did that come about? If you took 15 minutes each day to learn more *facts* about Vietnam, easily obtainable from the library or from available new sources, I guarantee that in a short time you will know more than many of the people who talk to me about it. How big is it? How many people live there? Did China ever rule over it? When? Is there any Chinese influence remaining and if so, is it pro-China or anti-China? I am not discussing with you the grave questions which are concerned with the Vietnam problem. I am suggesting that none of these questions can even be approached, let alone answered without basic knowledge of the geography and history of that area, and the facts you should know, you can learn in 15 minutes a day in just a few days.

We are here tonight to rejoice with the boys and with the parents and friends of the boys who have won the right to be called Eagle Scouts. I suspect that to be an Eagle Scout you must waste less time, and spend more time productively than the boys who do not aspire to be in that distinguished group. One of the astronauts now in orbit was an Eagle Scout. I have heard a Superintendent of the United States Military Academy at West Point say that he is always pleased when he finds that newly entering cadets are Eagle Scouts, because he knows that they have learned self discipline, and that the many skills evidenced by their merit badges were developed by careful attention to priorities, including the proper use of their spare time. I was present when the Commanding General of the Second United

States Army in the South Pacific, in World War II, was holding a conference, part of which was to determine whether or not to send a separate task force to a distant island. He wanted to do it but was looking for a commander. His chief of staff suggested a name, and the general got out the reference book of regular army officers, and looked him up. I recall very clearly hearing him read out a number of lines describing this officer, and then saying: "This is a good man. I note also that he was an Eagle Scout before he entered the academy, and I have found that boys who start that way usually measure up".

Do you know how long it takes to write a short letter or note? Ten minutes. Most people put off writing letters because they anticipate a long epistle, full of lots of things. Some of the best letters are short. Post cards are short. When you take a little trip, do you write to anyone? If you do, it is appreciated more for the fact that you thought of that person than for what you said. And ten minutes can always be found. The men in service consider receiving mail as the most important event of the week or day. Why? Well, they are not with their families and old friends and they want to feel close to them. Surrounded by their buddies, they are nevertheless lonesome.

I have not forgotten that although I twisted this subject out of its context, it nevertheless meant very plainly "ten or 15 minutes" and so I want to add just one more comment to these brief remarks.

Every Scout says the Scout law. He says that a Scout is loyal, a Scout is kind, and a Scout is reverent. It occurs to me that those words must mean more than so much printer's ink or they would not have been said over and over again by hundreds of thousands of Scouts for many generations.

Right now, there are several thousand young men serving in the Armed Forces, and many of them are engaged in combat against as clever, bold, resourceful and utterly ruthless opponents as we have ever encountered. We are suffering casualties, every day. Every day the bell tolls. And every time the bell tolls, it tolls for you too for you are involved.

I don't know what your individual religious affiliations are, but every one of you and every service man is a child of God, and I urge you to pray for them. Here is the finest service you can render. Here is the most rewarding five minutes or more that you can experience. You don't have to pray in church. Your prayers are to God, who is always listening. I want to quote to you some words from a service man, made just as he was departing for a troop ship to Vietnam.*(5) He was talking to children- his, and some near relatives. He said:

"I think I stand a good chance of coming back but this is a thing that has to be done, and I'm glad that I have had the training for this type of combat. My greatest hope is that I may bring back all the men in my company." He also says, "Pray for me, too. You may not think it means much now, but someday you will. I recall some lines from a poem by Tennyson that I read in Campbell School somewhere along about the sixth grade. I don't have the book with me but I remember it somewhat.

If thou shouldst never see my face again, pray for my soul. More things are wrought by prayer than this world dreams of. Wherefore, let thy voice rise like a fountain for me night and day. For what are men better than sheep or goats that nourish a blind life within the brain, if, knowing God, they lift not hands of prayer both for themselves and those who call them friend. For so the whole round earth is every way bound by gold chains about the feet of God."

A Scout is loyal, he is kind, and he is reverent. I am happy to be with you tonight and to express my appreciation for the fine work some of you have done in rising to the grade of Eagle Scout, and to encourage the other Scouts who are here to go on and realize the same achievement. And for all of you, I beg that you will devote an occasional ten or 15 minutes of your spare time to doing some of the things I have suggested, but above all that individually and collectively you pray for God's grace and mercy on our servicemen.

MEMORIAL DAY
Oberlin, Ohio, May 30, 1967

In 1863, just over one hundred years ago, several women visited the graves of their sons and husbands who had died in the service of the Confederacy, in Columbus, Mississippi. When they had finished decorating these graves of their loved ones, they looked over at the graves of the Union soldiers who were also buried there, and found them unattended, drab and forgotten. Unable to ignore the graves of the fallen Northern men, they carefully decorated those graves until there was nothing to distinguish them from all the others. Just one hundred years ago.

This, and similar incidents, touched the hearts of the whole Nation, giving hope that a Nation torn asunder by civil war might once again be united in spirit. In response to the gracious gesture of these Southern women, the Union's veteran organization inaugurated May 30th, as Decoration Day. Ceremonies were sponsored throughout the North while similar occasions were held independently in the South.

Five years later, Decoration Day became known as Memorial Day, a more fitting description of the day we now set apart as a salute to our military dead from all wars. In cemeteries and public places all over the Nation, groups such as this one are doing today what we do here. Many of us here today are veterans of one or more wars. Any man who has been engaged in battle has great respect for those who were his buddies, whether known to him personally or as simply a member of the Armed Forces, for in such circumstances we were all buddies. We were buddies not just because we live together, worked together and sweated it out together, but because we relied on each other. Several highly gifted military writers have advanced the theory that courage in a soldier comes only in part from his single minded resolve. Much of it springs from his respect for his buddies and his need to have and keep their respect. Whether a man is a sentry on a lonely outpost, or is in the midst of a combat group, he knows that others rely upon him to give a warning, to protect a flank, to cover a piece of the front, to man his part of the ship, or to navigate a plane. If there is any one dominant factor which motivates a man in the military service more than any other factor, it is the recognition of mutual reliance.

Mutual reliance. The expression is similar to responsibility, but the meaning is different. There is no aspect of military service which does not encompass the idea of mutuality, for even when a man finds himself alone and there is nobody around him, or those who are there are no longer able to fight, it is then the soldier remains a soldier because of his conviction that he still owes a duty to his buddies. You service men who are here know this.

Every deceased veteran has experienced this feeling and it is therefore in this sense that we can thoughtfully and correctly think of heroes when we assemble on Memorial Day. It is in this sense that we can read the words of John Donne: "Any man's death diminishes me, because I am involved in mankind, and therefore never send to know for whom the bell tolls; it tolls for thee."

I suppose that men have pondered on the meaning of existence since they were able to think, and when they learned how to write, they wrote about it. Many generations ago a man named Grotius wrote about war and peace. He considered how man would act in a state of nature unaffected by other human beings. If there was a first man on this earth, maybe his name was Adam, the only person in the whole world of any importance was Adam, because he was the only one. If there is a hermit today, although I don't know just where he would be found because of the shortage of unoccupied real estate, he undoubtedly thinks in terms of his own survival and pleasure. Even in Grotius' day the world was slowly filling up with people. He wrote a book entitled *De Jura Belli et Pacis,* concerning war and peace, because he recognized the need for some way to end the pointless conflicts being waged all around him and in all of the history he could read.

The story is told of a wealthy Frenchman, who looked about him in the late 1930s and found nothing promising. In fact, he looked at Hitler and thought of the many wars between Frenchmen and Germans and undertook to place his family in absolute security. He searched the face of the earth and finally found the ideal spot. Beautiful and undisturbed. A place where he could grow coconuts and live in shelter and peace. He moved his family, built a house, planted a grove, admired the sunset and relaxed. The place where he established his ideal residence was a little island called Guadalcanal. No place to hide.

I don't know when peace will dominate the hearts of men, or if it ever will, but I know that until it does, I need somebody to protect me. I live in one house. I occupy a small space in one city in one county in one state; but look who protects me when I need it. First, there is a telephone, and somebody on the other end to answer my summons; the local police, the county sheriff, the State of Ohio and the FBI. All of these are of no value whatsoever against a foreign aggressor who lusts for the riches of America. So we have our Armed Forces. We have had military protection all our lives and I pray the day will never come when we do not have it, until peace pervades the hearts of mankind.

Grotius thought that a system of international law could be worked out. In fact, he *found* international law in the many devices which nations used to keep the peace when they tried. But Grotius admitted the facts and therefore much of his great work was devoted to the rights and duties of neutrals which meant, of course, there had to be warring opponents or there would be no neutrals.

We must admit the facts today, too. My purpose is not to expound on the several theories of government or the positions which are taken today by the leaders of the world's nations. My purpose is to thank God we have had the protection of generations of men who took up arms for this country when they were asked to do so. This is a day we can express our gratitude to those who died for us and our families. I shall not press upon you my views as to why we are in Viet Nam or how to emerge from it. I do know, however, that our servicemen in Viet Nam are as highly motivated as any servicemen have ever been in any war we have been engaged. Furthermore, their training is better, their equipment is superior to any we have ever had, and their medical attention and supply are superb. We are all touched and impressed with the way in which our men have identified with the miseries and needs of the Vietnamese people and have responded with kindness and personal care and attention. We can be very proud of them.

PIGS
October 4, 1968

The suina is comprised of three families: the Dicotylidae, the Hippopotamidae and the Suidae. They have tubercles on the molar teeth and there is not found a complete fusion of the third and fourth metapodials in them to form a canon bone. One form of the Suidae family is an ungulate of the sub-order artiodactyla. This careful explanation is given so that you will never fail to recognize the animals before whom you should not cast your pearls "lest they trample them under your feet and turn again and rend you." Another name is swine. An easier name to remember is "pig"- which is my subject today.

Many years ago, when I was a small boy, my father, who was a busy lawyer, tried to satisfy a yearning to commune with nature by purchasing a small farm near Huron. He bought overalls and a straw hat and every Saturday afternoon he pitched hay or hoed corn. Many an evening was spent in research on agricultural matters, including the care, feeding, breeding and marketing of Poland China hogs. I was a part of all this because I worked on the farm during the summers and participated in the evening discussions. I should add, that except for Saturday afternoons and many evenings, my father worked harder than ever as a busy lawyer, for now he had not only a family to support, but also a farm. My father, you will have gathered, was not a farmer. A farmer is a man who works long, hard hours all week so he can go shopping in town on Saturday. My father was an agriculturalist. An agriculturalist is a man who spends his time at gainful employment, to acquire the money to spend on the farm.

Many memories of those days remain with me. We purchased a pure bred Poland China boar for $3,000. He came well recommended, for he had sired many offspring. In fact, so many offspring had he sponsored, that his prowess was attenuated, and he was sold after eighteen months, for $5. This is where I received my first lesson in the difference between depreciation and obsolescence. I recall also a beautiful young gilt whose registered name was "Pretty Lady". She was carefully crated and sent off to Chicago to be bred with a famous boar called "The Clansman," for which William Wrigley had paid $25,000. In due time, Pretty Lady returned home with a contented smile, gave birth to one pig and promptly lay on it. This provided me with a demonstration of the theory of probabilities in the realm of agricultural economics.

Many years later my daughter married a young man whose business hours are taken with the purchase, processing, and marketing of more hogs than I thought there were in the whole United States. Now I think you will understand why, although I might be expected to discuss with you some of the aspects of our military posture, or the discourse upon the constitutionality of the Civil Rights Bill, I want to talk about "PIGS".

Historically, the genus suss includes the European wild boar, the Indian wild boar, the Andaman Islands boar, a type named salvanius from the foot of the Himalayas, and the Africanus and procus of Africa. The Indian wild boar stands 30 to 40 inches high while the salvanius is but 11 inches at the shoulder. The tusks extend up on either side of the face, through the nose but not the mouth, curve back to the forehead and then forward again- sometimes 14 inches long. Wild pigs are now found only in the Old World. In the United States, the only real wild pig is the peccary, which is an entirely different family. Our modern breeds probably derive from the North European scrota, and also from the Malayan pigs, the vitatus. The pig was domesticated later than cattle or sheep, but earlier than the horse. Hogs in the United States are from selective breeding in this country and have such names as Duroc-Jersey, Poland China, and Chester White or Berkshire- strictly American creations. All our larger farm animals belong to one order- the ungulates, or hoofed animals. Of these, the pig was selected for his ability to fatten rapidly, and economically, and is the foremost means of converting feed into meat.

There was a time when pigs were regarded as easy feeders- in fact, they were permitted to be scavengers because they were not fastidious about food and they were easy keepers, especially for the marginal farmer. Some of you may recall that municipal garbage used to be sold to hog feeders. No longer are there such goings on. Quite aside from modern sanitary regulations, the science of feeding hogs for the production of the highest demand meat product in this and most countries has made it uneconomical and non-competitive to feed other than balanced rations of high quality food products.

Perhaps the ancient connotation of the word "swine" evokes a little prejudice. Perhaps someone believes that swine still retain the devils that according to the Biblical story, were said to enter them when cast out of men. This is a mistake, because all the swine into whom the devils entered, ran into the sea and presumably were drowned. Possibly the prejudice comes from the name of this animal. Perhaps I should have started with the familiar exhortation "O be some other name. What's in a name? That which we call a rose by any other name would smell as sweet."

When Farmer Jones considers all the possibilities of operating his farm, he wonders whether to raise pigs. He knows that there will always be a market. No longer are pigs considered a sort of collateral off-shoot of agriculture. Pigs are big business- protected with heated shelters, served with automatic feeders and waterers, inoculated against diseases, carefully inspected by government agents before they may be shipped between states, or even entered in many municipal markets. Pork contains all the food, chemical, hormone, vitamin, protein and fat content which the human body requires for its nourishment, and in addition, it is usually cheaper than other kinds of meat. With demand assured, the farmer wants only to know how profitable it will be for him to raise pigs instead of something else.

He starts out with feeder pigs, which he buys at about 40 pounds, and feeds them to maturity. The cost of buying feeder pigs, handling them, and feeding them, compared with what he will sell them for, is the problem he must solve. He may decide to breed them, in which case he will purchase boars and sows. The importance of good breeder stock is well known. He may purchase registered animals, whose pedigrees indicate that their ancestors were good producers, and if he does this, he will pay more for them. If he is a careful farmer, he will keep careful records, to include the cost of the brood sow and her maintenance from the time she is bred to the weaning of her pigs, how many pigs there are in the litter, how many of them live, how long it takes for them to reach market weight, and how much it costs. He will debate the proper time to market them hoping to get the best prices. The western hog rancher was for years accustomed to raising but one litter per year, most of which would reach market weight at the same time, with the obvious result that the market would be heavy with hogs. The middle western and eastern hog raiser, on the other hand, is used to raising two litters per year, in which case, the winter pigs must be more carefully protected lest the young pigs die from the cold. Every element of cost and marketing must be considered by the careful farmer, including some of the unknowns, such as weather, illness, and the cost of feed. Perhaps the most important element is the cost of corn, for traditionally, pigs eat the corn the farmer grows. If he can feed his corn to pigs, and get more from the pigs than he would get for the corn, he will raise pigs, but if he can sell the corn for more money than he will receive for the pigs that the corn would feed, he will not raise pigs. It takes about eleven months from the time a sow is bred until the pigs are ready for market, so the pig farmer must have a crystal ball. The feed problem is called the corn-hog ratio. It is calculated by determining the cost of the corn required to put 100 pounds on a pig, as compared with the market price of 100 pounds of live pig. Today, October 4, 1968, 220 pound pigs bring about $21 per hundredweight, and corn is worth about $1.10 per bushel.

Dividing $21 by $1.10, we find it takes 19 bushels of corn to equal the market price of 100 pounds of pig. If he has to feed 19 bushels of corn for each 100 pounds of pig weight, it is a standoff, but if the corn-hog ratio is 19 to 1 and the farmer can produce 100 pounds of pig with say, 11 bushels, which is the traditional normal ratio, then it may be to his advantage to raise pigs. If he is producing a superior market brand of pig which brings a premium price or is an easier feeder requiring less corn, he will make more profit. With 11 pounds at $1.10 ($12.10) and hogs at $21 per hundredweight, the farmer would get $1.91 per pound for his corn.

I then read another article in a trade journal, where careful records indicated a pig-corn ratio equivalent to $3.10 per bushel of corn, against the then current market price of $1.12. Lest everyone in this room consider throwing up his job and going into the pig business, let's look at a few other factors. In the same trade journal, one of the big commercial hog raisers calculated that his total cost, including depreciation on his investment and management expenses, averaged $.20 per pound. This also included an excellent registered breeding herd and high quality facilities, with automation. The current market price is $.21. If he was honest about it, he was making $.10 per pound, or $22 per hog. Perhaps he was getting premium prices for extra fancy pigs or perhaps he included profit in his cost. There are so many factors to consider that the corn-hog ratio is only one of them. For example, the cost of labor is up, and if it is replaced on the farm by automated feeding, watering, and cleaning lines, there must be a substantial capital investment. The farmer's time ought to be worth something, even if he is careless about evaluating it. The story is told about a farmer who was seen trying to back a gilt into a shipping crate. The harder he tried, the more obstinate and slippery was the pig. Time after time, the farmer got one hand on the left side, the other hand on an ear, and one foot in front, only to have the pig wiggle free. Finally a bystander asked him if it wouldn't save time to put the pig in head first. The farmer replied, "Hell, what's time to a hog?"

Recently I read a news story about a half million dollar automated hog farm that was lying idle. It had all the automatic scientific gadgets that there are. Why was it idle? The answer was there for all to see. The land didn't fail. The equipment worked very well. The hogs were willing to cooperate. The missing factor was man. Investigation by the non-resident owner disclosed that on one occasion the pigs were not fed or watered for 48 hours because everything was so automatic and so easy that the manager went fishing and forgot to set the automatic timer. During one week over fifty sows farrowed and there was no one in attendance. If pigs are born out in the barnyard, they usually survive if the weather is moderate, but in a fancy automated hog house with sterile hard floors, the little helpless pigs get squashed when their mothers lie down. Someone has to push a button to start the endless belt that brings in the straw. Someone has to watch how it is dumped in the pens. Someone has to supervise the mechanical scrapers so that the little pigs are not removed with the waste- and no one was there. The owner of this magnificent pork factory may have received some consolation from humming two lines from an old hymn: "Where every prospect pleases and only man is vile."

Automation on the farm is a subject I could develop, if there were time. To introduce the subject, where it pertains to hogs, let me mention some of the equipment and appliances now being advertised in trade journals:

1. A high pressure compressed air cleaner. Cost $260.
2. Steel slotted hog floors for the hog house. U.S. Steel Corporation.
3. A packaged hog house for 144 hogs, with insulation and automatic ventilation, automatic window openers, automatic water system, an auger shaped self-feeding system, slatted concrete floors, all for $4,527.

4. Nine different kinds of automatic water systems for field and shelter.
5. Infra-red gas operated brooder heater. Dries off new born pigs and keeps them warm. Automatic controls.
6. A portable electric heater, with blower and automatic thermostats delivering 200,000 BTUs all for $298.
7. Front end loader for the farm tractor, to handle loads around the pig houses.
8. An automatic milking machine to extract milk from sows for laboratory purposes, or to wet-nurse other pigs.
9. A batch hopper bin with automatic scales. When enough feed is taken from the automatic mixer and dumped into the hopper bin with a front end loader, or by mechanical worm or auger type feeder, the scale registers and the hopper dumps into the automatic feeder, while the farmer goes to the movies.
10. An automatic medicine proportioner which adds antibiotics to the water or feed in just the right proportions.
11. A hog sorter, shaped like a ladder on its side, with adjustable rungs. You chase all the hogs against the ladder, and only those that fit will go through. By using five ladders you get five different sizes in one steeplechase, like grading peaches.
12. Automatic overhead mixer and feeder that proportions the several feeds being used, and then when the timer goes off the right feed mixture is delivered to each section of the hog house and dumped in the troughs.
13. Hog squeezer. Holds the hog between side-bars while the farmer administers medicines or otherwise deals with piggy.

On Law and Country 161

14. Automatic hog oiler and insect killer. Consists of a post with several projections. When the pig rubs against it to scratch himself, the medicated oil anoints him where it itches.
15. Under floor manure collector automatically removes pig manure that drops between the slats of the floor whenever the accumulated weight indicates that removal is desirable.
16. Power actuated breeding crate supports a big boar while servicing a small gilt. Has push button controls.

Farmers must want to raise pigs or they wouldn't do it. Commercial hog raisers are successful, or they would not invest great sums in capital improvements. The fact is, pig raising is no different than making automobiles, overalls, radios, soap, or sewing machines. There is a market for all of these things, but the requirements are capital, labor, skill, and responsible management. I suppose there will always be subsistence level farmers, but to be an active member of our agricultural complex, the successful farmer must graduate from a college of agriculture and be an educated leader. The new farmer today not only can supervise the hired hand, but he can solve some of his most important problems with calculus, and I suspect the day is not far off when the manager of a great farm complex will be able to program a computer. I might add here that the suburban home owner with twenty feet of tomatoes, radishes and lettuce would not have the merit to attempt to advise the professional market gardener, but marginal farmers are many, and they all vote.

Well, this little pig has gone to market- a sleek 220 pound hog, inoculated against disease, tuberculin tested, fed and watered right up to the packing house door. There it will be despatched painlessly with an electric stunning machine, and thereafter separated into marketable units. From here on we are no longer concerned with pigs but with commercial products. What does the packer have, and what does he do with it?

First, he will have bought the animal by weight. The packing house will produce a carcass, which will be sold as a carcass or it will be separated into market cuts. The carcass will weigh about 70% of the live weight. The other 30%, which includes the hair and the "innards" and contains both edible and inedible parts, will be sold for about $1.95. 30% of a 220 pound hog is 66 pounds. The packer paid $.21 per pound, and sold it for $.03 per pound, or a net loss of $.18 or $11.88 on nearly 1/3 of his hog.

In fact, the packer seldom will operate at a 1% profit. The national average is 6/10 of 1%. The packer does not have adequate working capital; he must borrow it, and pay for the use of the money. If he sells for cash, his interest cost will be less, but if he sells on credit, not only is his working capital tied up for a time, but he runs the risk of credit losses. This is not a small problem. Meat processors buy by the truckload. One truckload of hog carcasses represents an investment of nearly $10,000. Just one of the Sandusky packers kills up to 10,000 hogs per week, or $450,000 worth.

The meat processor must pay the shipping cost and pass it on to the retailer. The retailer will add 24% to 25% as his markup and the housewife acquires the end product. There is a great deal more involved in this operation. I have only discussed fresh pork. However, much of what you buy will be smoked, cured or otherwise precessed, and all of this requires the expenditure of capital and labor.

It is interesting to note a hog carcass consists basically of four primal cuts: the loin, the shoulder, the ham and the belly. This represents 46% of the live weight. Let us trace some of this product.

Recently a whole pork loin roast was advertised for $.68 per pound. Starting with a 220 pound live hog, for which the farmer received $.21 per pound, the loin represents 14.75% of the carcass weight. The carcass weight is 70% of the live weight. Therefore, the loin is 10% of the live weight or 22 pounds. The difference between what the farmer received per pound and what the housewife pays per pound for this loin is $.47. For this $.47, the hog is slaughtered, inspected by the U.S. Government Department of Agriculture, chilled in a refrigerated cooler, shipped on a refrigerated truck to a processor, separated into a usable loin in a federally inspected plant, cut into smaller portions, shipped to a retailer who stores it in a clean refrigerated case, advertises it in a newspaper, trims off the extra fat and cuts it to the size desired, wraps it, and hands it to the customer. It sounds as though someone had made 300% gross profit. Has he? Starting with the live hog, 30% of it is worth $.03 per pound. When the farmer received $.21 per pound, it is true that he received only $.21 for a $.68 loin, but he also sold $.03 bone, fat and offal and was paid by federal inspections for the packer's shrinkage and the condemnations of diseased animals.

When you buy bacon or ham, you get it processed in one of many possible ways. It will be cured, smoked, trimmed, boned, packaged, aged, even partially cooked- however you want it. If you buy it by brand, such as Daisyfield, which is the J.H. Routh Packing Company brand in Sandusky, you will find it carefully packaged and labelled, but you will also expect to receive the same product every time you buy that brand, which requires grading and uniformity of selection and packing. This in turn requires the use of similar hogs. It used to be that the more a hog weighed, the more money it brought. This is not true. Of course a hog is sold by weight, but the hog buyer selects the animals with care and will pay more for a lean or meat type hog because be knows that meat will bring more than fat.

As a hog gets fatter and fatter he is worth less. A hog weighing over 250 pounds will often bring less than one weighing around 200, although it costs substantially more for the farmer to put on the extra weight. Incidentally, this explains in part what happened to the National Farmers Organization and its hog strike, withholding hogs from the market to make the price rise. The price went up for a short time, but the hogs being withheld from the market were eating and their weight was increasing, so that when they finally reached the market, their value was lower.

So now we are back to the farmer who not only must decide whether he wants to raise pigs, but if he does, what kind of pigs and where he can get them as feeder stock, or what breeder stock must be acquired if he raises them. It must be even more apparent by this time that the subsistence or marginal farmer will not prosper. The technology of meat production cannot be understood by the backwoods farmer with forty acres and no education. I could prolong these remarks by discussing the difference between the entrepreneur in agriculture who collectively has a huge vote and a government subsidy, and the merchant or manufacturer who bucks the competitive technology of his specialty, and either wins or goes bankrupt in the process. However, in a study recently completed by Chase Manhattan Bank the number of farm proprietors since 1948 has dropped 50%, while in the same period the number of non-farm business owners has dropped about 9%.

It is often supposed that pork will not keep as well as other meats. This is true because the meat is softer, and of course in olden days, especially in the hot Holy Land, pork was forbidden for religious reasons which actually had their basis in the climate. Even a few years ago, most pork found in the butcher shops came from near-by packing houses. Today, with modern refrigeration, both the preservation problems and the mileage are overcome. As many as two thousand hogs per day are often shipped from Sandusky to processors on the Eastern Sea Board. A truck will leave here in the afternoon and be at the processor's plant by five o'clock in the morning, in time for the first shift. One truck will hold over 200 carcasses, plus many boxes of cut pork products. Other trucks leave later in the day, so that the New York area, for example, receives a substantial part of its pork products from Sandusky, Ohio, competitively with other points of origin.

A word should be said about trichinosis, a hog disease which can affect man, and which is much feared. There is one sure and certain way to avoid this problem and it is almost impossible not to avoid it except with the rankest kind of carelessness. The trichinella spiralis is always killed at a temperature of 137° Fahrenheit. There has not been a case of trichinosis in the army for 35 years. There is no recipe using pork which calls for a cooked temperature as low as 137°. Most recipes call for interior heats of 160° to 165°. Aside from all this, if the pink color of pork has turned to gray, which happens between 160° and 165°, the meat will automatically have reached a point well beyond the danger of trichinosis.

Finally, it is interesting to note a learned article on the subject of arterio-sclerosis in which the writer claims that it is possible that polyunsaturated fats may accelerate arterio-sclerosis, contrary to popular advertising. He bases his argument on the discovery that in persons having severe arterio-sclerosis, the artery walls have a consistently greater polyunsaturated fatty acid content than do the walls of normal arteries where the saturated fatty acids are decreased. He then quoted the American Medical Association as saying that the present anti-fat, anti-cholesterol fad may involve some risk. The author is the director of nutrition research for the National Live Stock and Meat Board. He says there is some evidence that as the blood cholesterol lowers with the use of polyunsaturated fats, there is an increase in the cholesterol content of the blood vessel walls, heart muscle and other tissues.

I'm not a scientist, but of all the food tips I can give you about pigs, one is real good. The vitamin that keeps the nervous system in order is thiamine, and pork is the key source of thiamine in the diet. It is THE thiamine food. A pork chop a day keeps the psychiatrist away.

Charles Lamb - The Essays of Elia - Dissertation on Roast Pig:

> Pig- let me speak his praise- is no less provocative of the appetite, than he is satisfactory to the criticalness of the censorious palate. The strong man may batten on him, and the weakling refuseth not his mild juices.

Unlike to man's mixed characters, a bundle of virtues and vices, inextricably inter-twisted, and not to be unravelled without hazard, he is- good throughout. No part of him is better or worse than another. He helpeth, as far as his little means extend, all around. He is the least envious of banquets. He is all neighbor's fare.

PEARL HARBOR DAY
Sandusky, Ohio
Sunday, December 7, 1969

Twenty eight years ago today, American sailors, soldiers and airmen were killed or wounded when the Japanese air force bombed Pearl Harbor.

We are all products of our environment. History is made by men, who live, and die, doing the things they must do in response to the demands which society makes upon them. The way in which those soldiers, sailors, marines and airmen met their responsibilities on December 7, 1941, must be judged in relationship to the social forces which *they* experienced.

The historian has many roles. One of them is the duty to portray men and events in the light of the circumstances which surrounded them. This is not easy. Every person here today who is under 28 years was not yet born on Pearl Harbor Day. Every person here who is not yet 46 years old was not in World War II combat because he would not have been 18 years old when the war was over. A person who has never worn a uniform in a war can never fully comprehend what it is like, and those who were then unborn will never understand it at all.

Most of us who are here today have worn a uniform in wartime. We know what the state of mind America was in at that time. We know what enormous burdens were placed on our servicemen, because our society required it of them. Those men did what they were supposed to do, and no man can deny the title of hero to anyone who meets responsibility head-on and gives his life doing it.

The American Veterans of World War II have long chosen the anniversaries of Pearl Harbor to recall to themselves, to service men generally, and to the nation, the tragic event which triggered the biggest war in history. But when we do this, we also recall the long drawn-out conferences, with representatives of Japan in Washington, which preceded their perfidious act.

We recall that all of us, including our representatives at the State Department in Washington at that time, insisted that Armistice Day in *1918* was the end of great wars- that reasonable men could reconcile their differences at the conference table- and so we conferred and negotiated- and then learned that while these efforts to effect peaceful reconciliation of differences were being made, the Japanese Navy was already en route toward Pearl Harbor. It was indeed a day that will live in infamy.

There is a strange familiarity about these words. Do you recall that Neville Chamberlain came home from Munich, where there was also a bargaining table and said that there will be peace in our time? Do you remember the words of Winston Churchill, at Neville Chamberlain's funeral? "Whatever else history may or may not say about these terrible, tremendous years, we can be sure that Neville Chamberlain acted with perfect sincerity according to his lights and strove to the utmost of his capacity and authority to save the world from the struggle in which we are now engaged." And do you recall that in 1917, President Wilson said, "We are too proud to fight?" Do you recall the hundreds of days of Panmujon, where nothing happened but talk; where one side engaged in nothing but vituperation for months?

Do you find any similarity at Paris? Today?

None of the men in uniform at Pearl Harbor were at the conference tables. None of you were there either. The interaction of violent forces, led by a maniac in Germany, and by warlords in Japan, swept aside the good will of others.

These conferences, these talks, these negotiations, these fervent appeals to reason- they have been initiated by, and represent the ideal of the leaders of our country, for such has been the historical American pattern. Where we have been wrong- and God help us, there have been times when we were wrong, we were nevertheless confronting the wrong-doer, we were helping the weak, the war torn, the oppressed.

On Law and Country 169

At the time of Pearl Harbor we were militarily weak. We had only started to expand our armed forces, and after Pearl Harbor the whole world shuddered at the destruction of a major part of our navy. But some of our men were there. Few they were, but they stood up for our country- and many of them died for it. We shall never doubt the courage, the fortitude, the pride- and the integrity- I repeat, the *integrity* of the men in uniform.

We have been shocked at recent disclosures of fatalities among civilians in Vietnam. (The My Lai incident- R.W.R.) Most of us here have worn the uniform and we did not experience such things. I don't know what we shall learn of those events of last year, but I do know that America is one of the very few nations in the world which attempts to impose a moral code on their armed forces. Battlefield atrocities are not typical of the American soldier. He knows that the Armed Forces Code of Conduct is not a set of rules, but is our way of life, and that it must be honored even when his enemy sneers at it. Here are the words of an editorial I recently read.

> "The Vietnamese people, north and south, have historically lived by a different warfare code. Hanoi's legions are buttressed by modern theories of Maoist revolution, and their battlefield conduct often seems barbaric. They consider the ceremonial torture of prisoners or civilians to be an extension of the struggle, and they regularly indulge in wildly irresponsible lies about American conduct. American national philosophy demands that we shall first be true to ourselves. Our military men are strong enough to acknowledge this fact, and they accept civilian investigation into allegations of misbehavior. They should be spared the inequity of sanctimonious exposure by partisan elements who dream of stopping the war by humiliating the military establishment. Such misguided leaders will only drive military leaders

into the equally unqualified arms of the bellicose war-hawk element in our government, thus politicizing our armed forces and destroying the military ethic of submission to national authority. The very fact that the recent allegations are being brought into a court of law proves that we do adhere to our own standards of discipline and disproves the taunts of those who enjoy harassing the professional soldier. Patriotism in America is fortified by truth, not by burying our misdeeds in a red, white and blue cloak of self-righteousness."

As an American soldier lately returned from Vietnam put it, "It is a painful task to watch in helpless rage while an enemy used women and children for shields as their snipers pick off American troops. But there are ways of countering the tactics of the dirty fighter. The rewards which accrue to the soldier who chooses the harder right over the easier wrong are not worn on the chest, but they are more durable and worthy. As long as there are American soldiers engaging in armed conflict, in any spot on the globe, they must answer to the highest standards of moral conduct known to the American people. Their actions must remain continuously open to legal review by citizens of highest integrity and impartiality. The traditions of the American man-at-arms are at stake, for ultimately *he* is all of *us*."*(6)

What do we say to all these things on Pearl Harbor Day? What do we say of the sailor who lies forever entombed in the hold of a battleship on the bottom of the bay at Pearl Harbor? Of the anti-aircraft gunner who died at Hickam Field? Of the pilot who flew his bomber straight into the smoke-stack of the Japanese cruiser? Of the men from Fort Clinton who died at Bataan?

What do we say of the marine who died in the rear guard action in Korea while he protected his buddies from hordes of Chinese Communists? Or of the American soldier from Sandusky who shares responsibility for the safety of his squad in Vietnam- on this Pearl Harbor Day?

Well I'll tell you what we say. We say that for so long as this world is inhabited by human beings and for so long as the *peace* of God continues to pass human understanding, for just that long there will be American soldiers- and sailors- and marines- and airmen- who will stand loyal to the death between their countrymen and their enemies: This is the meaning of Pearl Harbor Day.

TRIBUTE TO BRIGADIER GENERAL RICHARD McNELLY, 1971

Forty years ago, Richard Leeson McNelly and I were lieutenants in the horse-drawn field artillery, at Fort Knox, Kentucky.

Thirty years ago, we both entered the full-time military service with Ohio's 37th Division, and thereafter we served in the same or parallel units in the South Pacific throughout World War II.

Twenty-five years ago we both undertook assignments in the 83rd Reserve Division.

Ten years ago we both retired from the active reserve, in the same month; and for the past ten years we have kept in touch with each other.

I do not know any person in the military service who better exemplifies the soldierly qualities which I want to touch upon now. Dick McNelly had courage, and great drive, but let me mention some other qualities.

FIRST: He was responsible. As a commander or as a staff officer, whenever he received an assignment, he executed it in a superior manner. There were no loose ends. His plans were workable, they were successfully executed, and he saw them through to the finish.

SECOND: He had absolute integrity. He was one of that small number of this earth's inhabitants of whom it can be said that he was intuitively and intellectually honest.

THIRD: He was loyal. This is a more significant trait in a soldier than some may realize. In the intensely emotionally charged atmosphere that surrounds men in combat, any mistake, any small variation from the highest standard can cause anguish, even death. But soldiers are human beings, and they act like human beings. The kind of loyalty I refer to is the loyalty of a commander who stands up for his men, not only against the enemy, but in their defense against short tempered senior officers, and the loyalty of a staff officer who protects his own commander- the kind of loyalty which includes both duty and compassion.

FOURTH: He was a leader. He did not just give orders. When he told his men to do something, however dangerous, they believed that those orders were necessary, that they were given for good reasons- and they did their best to carry them out.

FIFTH: He was dedicated. For example, the individual units of his 637th Tank Destroyer Battalion were often attached to other organizations. I well remember when he had four companies attached to or supporting four different major organizations in four different parts of Northern Luzon at the same time. Colonel McNelly took his jeep all over the country to see that his men were fed and supplied, and to counsel with the company commanders, and to acquaint senior commanders with the fact that his units were there.

After World War II, General McNelly had an active and deeply sincere interest in attracting and training young men in the Organized Reserve. He knew that historically the Regular Army is never big enough to meet a major emergency, without a great reserve force of trained men to back it up.

When General McNelly died, the United States sustained a loss. His character, integrity, loyalty, leadership, and dedication to his country are the soldierly qualities without which a nation cannot survive, but with these qualities our soldiers can protect and defend the country that General McNelly loved so well.

Let us sum it up in the words of Daniel Webster, who said:

> I was born an American; I live an American; I shall die an American; and I intend to perform the duties incumbent upon me in that character to

the end of my career. I mean to do this with absolute disregard of personal consequences... What is the individual man, with all the good or evil that may betide him, in comparison with the good or evil which may befall a great country, and in the midst of great transactions which concern that country's fate? Let the consequences be what they will, I am careless. No man can suffer too much, and no man can fall too soon, if he suffer, or if he fall, in the defense of the liberties and constitution of his country.

MEMORIAL DAY
Sandusky, May 1971

Among the great calamities of history, none more seriously affected the people of one nation than did our War Between the States. Three years after it ceased, and while the South was undergoing the anguish of Reconstruction, several women visited the graves of their sons and husbands and brothers in Columbus, Mississippi. When they finished decorating the graves of their loved ones who had fallen under the banner of the Stars and Bars, the symbol of the Confederacy, they noticed other graves, unattended, covered with weeds, forlorn and forgotten. There lay Union soldiers.

These women were unable to ignore them, and so they decorated them carefully, until there was nothing to distinguish all the graves. This gracious gesture of these Southern women touched the hearts of the Nation, giving hope that a Nation torn apart by civil war might again be united in spirit. A Union veterans' organization inaugurated Decoration Day. Five years later it became Memorial Day- and ever since that beginning, people have assembled in cemeteries in May and have decorated the graves of the veterans of all wars.

Look around you. Off in the southeast corner is the Veterans Circle. Down the main road to the west is another plot set apart for veterans. Scattered all over the cemetery are the graves of men who have served in the Army, the Navy, the Marine Corps, the Air Force. There is a marker, and a small but beautiful symbol- the Flag.

However, this is Erie County, in the State of Ohio and the United States of America, and you can *count* the veterans' graves in this cemetery. If this were France, or Germany, or Belgium, or Poland or Czechoslovakia, this would be a huge cemetery, and the number of veteran graves would be practically countless. At first we were protected by thousands of miles of ocean. In the beginning, we established our independence by means of the heroism of the Continental Army. Later, by a combination of the Monroe Doctrine and a veteran Union Army, a great European power gave up the idea of supporting Maximilian, and establishing a power base on the American continent. Still later, and rather easily, we persuaded Spain to relinquish its grasp on Cuba.

Still later, as the world became smaller, and its peoples began to know each other, we joined with other allies in Europe to stop world domination by an aggressive Imperial Germany. And still the world shrank, and again we joined hands with other democratic societies to stop another gigantic threat from Hitler and from the Japanese Empire. The men who stopped these military giants lie in cemeteries like this one. Our purpose here is to unite in paying tribute to our countrymen who made it possible for us to be here, in Sandusky, Ohio on this lovely day in May 1971. We must take care lest we become so involved in the uncertainties and frustrations of the Asian conflict, that we lose our perspective, become embittered and allow our emotions to rule our hearts.

We are *not* here today to debate the current issues. This is not Election Day. This is Memorial Day. The men to whom we pay our respects today *died* in the service of our country. Most of them were civilians, who became soldiers or sailors or airmen or marines because they were needed. Most of then were not professional soldiers. They entered training camps and learned how to serve, for the time of the emergency. Their training was only as good as the capabilities of the professionals who trained them. Thank God it was enough. I have a very keen and personal recollection, in the days just before World War II, when we used stove pipes as simulated cannon, yes- stove pipes- and took trucks and painted the word "TANK" on the side of them. Somehow, between thousands of miles of protective oceans, and the preoccupation of our enemies with their immediate problems, and the passage of time, we made it. We had dedicated leadership, and superb career officers, but we made it essentially with a civilian army.

In the present state of the world, we do not dare to let down our guard, but I want that guard to come from the civilian population of the United States, who have received sufficient training that they can respond effectively if the need arises. In this day of sophisticated weaponry we must keep abreast of technological developments, or we will be out-classed. I do not for one moment believe that we dare trust the innate good nature or compassion of the leaders of the Soviet Socialist Republics, or of Red China. However, I *do* indeed believe that if we keep our guard up, and stay alert, and maintain the military essentials, all the peoples of the world, including our potential enemies, may come to realize that from here on no world war can ever be won, but it can be lost, and therefore, God willing, it will never be started.

And this brings me to a subject which has been giving me concern. We are living in a fast moving age. When I was a boy, my parents used to call on their friends, and they came to our house. Conversation ensued. To converse, one had to think, and there were lively discussions. More personal effort went into the formation of opinions than is the case today when everybody learns the news, and it interpretation, and how to think on every subject every hour on the hour, and twice every evening, from a news commentator or from TV pictures.

Let me say right now that I am not attacking the news media. Just think about it. On Mother's Day, millions remembered their mothers, but not under television lights. There was no headline such as "10,000,000 mothers receive Mothers Day cards." There are Memorial Day ceremonies all over the United States right at this hour and they are being reported and televised, but we also read about the number of automobile casualties predicted for the Memorial Day weekend. Every day, thousands of passengers are traveling across this country in airplanes, but a television crew does not set up a camera to show a little spot in the sky. It has to be that way. Well, news is something unusual, and that is what is in demand. What most of us do everyday would make a dull picture.

What concerns me is that the picture or story of crime or violence will crowd out of our minds the essential goodness of man and his daily deeds and thoughts. It's a matter of proportion of course, but it is quite possible to become so accustomed to pictures of hate and violence and selfishness and cruelty that we commence to wonder if the whole world is evil. And that's simply not true and you know it every day of your lives right here in Sandusky. And of all the horrible events that we most want to avoid it is another war. We here in this gathering owe our lives to the soldiers, sailors, marines and airmen who have stood between us and catastrophe, and have died. This is the essential goodness of the men we honor today- they gave their lives for us. We must give the most profound thought to ways and means of avoiding war, but we must never forget that when events overwhelmed us, and we were in peril, we were defended magnificently. By whom? Our servicemen, our own countrymen, our relatives, our friends, our brothers.

Three weeks ago I had occasion to visit the Armed Forces Staff College at Norfolk, Virginia. The students were an equal mix of officers from the Army, Navy, Marine Corps and Air Force- and some civilians. The officers were all senior majors or young lieutenant colonels, or the navy equivalent, between 36 and 40 years old. They were studying world affairs. I attended a seminar devoted to an examination of ways in which our officers, together with state department representatives and members of the Peace Corps, could help a South American country. The subjects discussed were roads, bridges, the improvements of river channels and barge canals, cultivation of the soil, improving cattle and hogs, and establishing better communications between cities and the back country. The emphasis was on ascertaining what the people need, and then figuring out how the United States could help them to get it. There was a time was when Washington D.C. knew all there was to know about everything, and whatever it thought best was best. Not any longer. The point of this seminar was how to listen, not how to tell. This is a new approach, and it is badly overdue. The instructors were mostly knowledgeable civilians, including people from the South American country with which they were concerned. The Armed Forces Staff College is probably unknown to you, but there they study history, geopolitics and sociology.

About half the student officers were graduates of Annapolis or West Point, and the other half were college graduates who had decided to enter one of the services. All of them had spent time in foreign countries. They are in the age bracket from which the leaders were selected at the beginning of World War II. I went to a family picnic with a group of them, and their wives and lots of children. They were talking about Boy Scout troops, life saving classes, the school system. They were keen, immensely interested in people, and a heart warming example of American citizens. Now why do I tell you about them?

Well, they do not appear on television, and you don't read about them, so your assessment of military personnel does not include this very significant segment of what they do. Of course they are part of the military defense system, upon which we must all rely for our security against aggression, but there is a general realization that although we must be prepared for war, the way to avoid misunderstandings which lead to wars, is to get to know the peoples of the world, and to help them- and that is what these fine young men are learning.

On Saturday, the President addressed the cadets at West Point. West Point is a college. Of course it is a military college and the cadets wear uniforms, but essentially it is a college. It is after graduation that the cadets attend branch service schools. These men, and their counterparts at Annapolis and the Air Force Academy constitute as fine a group of young people as there are. What they will do in the future, depends upon what the country asks them to do. The motivation with which these young men start out is Duty, Honor, Country.

More than half of all the officers in the Army come from civilian colleges, obtaining their commissions from the R.O.T.C.

This means that a major part of the Army's leadership comes from the college campuses, the same colleges which Erie County's High School graduates will attend. In fact, some of them are Army officers now. They and other college graduates exert a tremendous influence on the Army.

The military system of the United States will never go very far wrong if its leaders come from Ohio State and Bowling Green. These are the peoples' universities, your and their R.O.T.C. graduates will keep the Army the peoples' Army.

Now what does all of this mean on the last day of May 1971? Well, first, and fundamentally, we are alive and free because others have bought our freedom with their lives. Second, we have reached a point in time and perspective when wars and the thought of wars are so abhorrent that we will insist upon peace. We are now engaged in decelerating the pace of the Asiatic involvement. We yearn for the return of our troops, and it is no longer a matter of *whether* or not they will come home but *when*. Third, peace will not come because of the pleas of the weaklings of this world, but because the United States has the strength and the moral courage to insist upon it. Both of these conditions are essential. We *will* maintain our strength because we know we must. God help us if we let down our guard. And we have the moral fibre, because it is our heritage- from those veterans of all the wars who we honor on the Memorial Day.

Let us say with Ecclesiaticus: "Their bodies are buried in peace; but their name liveth for evermore."

MEMORIAL DAY
Oakland Cemetery, Sandusky
May 30, 1974

At the breakfast table I read a newspaper headline. It said: "Murder in the street. Clevelander becomes a routine statistic." There is a headline like that one every morning. It does not usher in a happy day. At the same breakfast table, I read another line from another publication. It said, "This is the day that the Lord has made. Let us rejoice and be glad in it."

If the second line were the only one I had read, the day would have started happily. Every day would start happily, because every day is a day the Lord has made.

This day is a day that the Lord has made and we can rejoice in it and be glad. Today we have grateful hearts as we pause to honor those inevitable men whose lives were exchanged for ours and our way of life.

The pause is brief, but significant, and the reasons for it are reassuring. Many years ago, a group of gracious Southern women were placing flowers on the graves of Confederate soldiers and noticed the near-by graves of Union soldiers, bare, drab, and untended in the midst of graves whose decorations evidenced the presence of love. The contrast was so apparent that the women were moved by compassion to lay flowers on the neglected graves. This occurred in 1863, at Columbus, Mississippi, right in the middle of the War between the States. The idea took hold and a group of women in Vicksburg decorated the graves of soldiers buried there. In 1865, the Stonewall Jackson Memorial Association was formed in Winchester, Virginia to decorate the graves in that area. That same year, General Logan, Commander in Chief of the Grand Army of the Republic, a Union Veterans' organization, laid plans for the decoration of graves. In 1868, special ceremonies were formally held in the National Cemetery at Arlington. The custom took hold and is now a national event taking place on what is now called Memorial Day, the last Monday in May.

Memorial Day is rooted in love, nourished by love of country and cherished in our hearts by love of God, to Whose everlasting arms we have committed our departed comrades. In Sandusky Bay, on Johnson's Island, is a beautiful cemetery well kept and maintained by the Federal government. All the graves are of Confederate soldiers who died in the military prison on the island. No longer is there bitterness or rancor between North and South. The War Between the States has been over for more than 100 years. The warring participants spoke the same language, had much of the same heritage, and were participants in the same earlier history. Ease of communication was no doubt the strongest factor in bringing us together, a factor which is missing in our relationship with the peoples of most of the nations of the world. The doctrine of the brotherhood of man should work between all human beings, but as a
matter of cold, hard fact, the first step is acquaintanceship, then friendship, then respect, and finally, love. We are still struggling to become acquainted.

Today the fallen of nine major wars rest in cemeteries in the United States and overseas. Their early battles were at Bunker Hill and Yorktown. Their last battles were fought in the Argonne Forest, on the Normandy beaches, on Pacific islands, on the hills of Korea and in the jungles of Vietnam. Although separated by time and distance, these places have one thing in common; they are reminders of the price we have paid worldwide for peace and freedom.

Those whose comprehension of war is not based on personal experience and limited to the Vietnam conflict may have acquired a repugnance to war which overshadows their personal awareness of the meaning of peace and of freedom. Although I am not presently aware of any great threat to the United States, at least not an imminent threat, I am nevertheless greatly concerned that the Soviet Union's naval strength and total weaponry may some day, perhaps even now, equal or exceed that of the United States, despite all the talk about detente, and high level conferences between our president and a Soviet leader and television views of diplomats embracing each other at the world's airports. I firmly believe that if, and whenever, the Soviet Union should determine that it could impose its will on the United States, it would, without the slightest regard for any prior promise or representation or any treaty. To it, the word "morals" means the victory of the proletariat. The achievement of that victory is the fulfillment of its highest moral obligation. The Communist does not consider himself a sinner, and you and I ought to be realistic about it. Where all the people and all the property are pooled and there is no God, there is no place for the peace of God or for the kinds of political morals that we recognize. Please don't mistake my attitude. I've been all through the McCarthy days and don't see Communists hiding in all the bushes. However, in the present state of world politics, we do not dare become weak. If we do, we should not come to a Memorial Day observance.

Why did our fallen veterans die for us? There is an inscription on a Confederate monument at Arlington that provides an answer: "Not for fame or reward- not for place or for rank- not lured by ambition or goaded by necessity- but in simple obedience to duty as they understood it, these men suffered all- sacrificed all- dared all- and died." Did they believe that theirs would be the last war and that it would end in permanent peace? We will never know.

The two most valued gifts one generation can give to another are peace and freedom. They are worth fighting for. They must be fought for, not just for our own enrichment, but for those who will come after us.

Our responsibilities are clear. We must complete the unfinished work of our heroic dead. We are fortunate to soon have a major event reminding us of our tasks. I refer to the National Bicentennial in 1976. This will afford us unique opportunities to note the steady growth of our country and the principles which guided it to world leadership. In 200 years, we have advanced from 13 colonies with 3 million people to a nation of 50 states and 205 million people. We have progressed from a four-week Atlantic crossing in 1776, to a three day trip to the moon. We have wealth, and the world's highest standard of living. We enjoy more freedom and we have more opportunities than any other people in the world.

When I started to speak today, I said that this is a day that the Lord has made. He will make tomorrow too, and all the future tomorrows. In calling to your attention the special significance of Memorial Day so that neither you nor I will inadvertently overlook the ideals of which that day is a reminder, I have quite deliberately dwelt upon the subjects of peace and freedom as affected by the risks of losing them to very powerful national interests which exclude God entirely in their concept of world society.

I have insisted that we remain strong, and in pursuing this argument I mentioned patriotism. Basically, a patriot is one who loves his own country. The word is derived from French and Latin words meaning countryman rather than pure geography. In as complicated a world as this one and in a democratic country where the people have the right of free speech, and we surely have *that*, people who criticize, loud and clear, and there are many of them, are sometimes accused of being unpatriotic. Where some course of action upon which our country has embarked is much criticized by many people, there is always the risk that they will be called unpatriotic, and if this happens often, the very word "patriotism" becomes suspect. When I used the word a few minutes ago, I was reminding all of us to distinguish carefully between criticism and disloyalty. At this very moment, in our country's daily happenings in Washington, there is probably more criticism than has been heard for generations, but that doesn't mean that we do not love our country, for our country is our people, and that includes you and me.

On Law and Country

When we criticize what is going on, we criticize the people who are responsible. In the Soviet Union and in China, this is as far as one can go. The highest leader is the limit, and the limit is human for he cannot ask for God's help. He doesn't know God, but you do and I do. All our coins say "In God we trust" which means this is a God fearing nation.

I want to leave this message with you today: God-loving people can elect God-loving leaders. God-loving leaders will turn to God for instructions and help, and in the greatness and wideness of God's love, He will care for and protect His people who call upon Him. That is why we never have to fear any Communist nation or group of nations. This is why we need not fear as long as we trust God, loud and clear, alone, with our families, wherever people gather together, and nationally.

Let us join the Psalmist who, three thousand years ago, sang: "Except the Lord build the house, they labour in vain that build it; except the Lord keep the city, the watchman waketh in vain." (Psalm 127:1)

ABOUT RUSSELL RAMSEY
Upon His Retirement as Director, Officer, Legal Counsel
Bechtel-McLaughlin Company After Twenty-Seven Years
Of Distinguished Service August 16, 1975

The admiration and affection that we all hold for Russell A. Ramsey cannot be expressed in the presentation of a material gift, however valuable.

The excellence of his thought and manner, plus the high level of his professional competence, have brought respect and dignity, as well as proper formality, to the management of the Corporation's affairs.

For a Company that specializes in adding brilliance and luster to basic materials, Russell did just that to the texture and tone of the deliberations of the Board of Directors where he subordinated his greater talents to act as Secretary. Likewise for the meeting of the stockholders. His Minutes of the meetings of Bechtel-McLaughlin- "ink," as he liked to call it, are masterpieces of official recording. What went into those Minutes as the formal action of the Corporation often were the result of Russell's own wise and knowledgeable counsel on the applicable elements of corporation law and decorum. When Russell took the floor to explain an obscure point of complex legal significance, we knew we were not only illuminated but were enjoying the privilege of listening to a fine teacher.

The personal prestige of General Ramsey lifted up the morale of our fledgling Company, gave us courage to persevere and added to our stature in the community.

To think that this fine and accomplished man gave willingly of himself to us all these years without rendering a bill is a tribute without comparison to high moral and spiritual motives. The fact that he is off to Gainesville, Florida, to assist his son in the conduct of a school for underprivileged boys is clinching evidence of the unique humanity of this man.

In saying goodbye and thank you to Russell, let us sincerely wish that God will bless him in all his endeavors.

"EXCHANGING THE PEACE"
Holy Trinity Episcopal Church Gainesville, Florida
July 20, 1979

Passing or exchanging the Peace was first introduced in the trial liturgy which preceded the Proposed Book of Common Prayer. When members of the congregation greeted each other with the words "The Peace of the Lord (be with you)," they had mingled feelings, which included some embarrassment. Episcopalians were not accustomed to talking that way with each other. It was explained that the rubric said: "The greeting, 'The Peace of the Lord be always with you' is addressed to the entire assembly. In the exchange between individuals which may follow, any appropriate words of greeting may be used." Now, after several years of passing the Peace to each other, one often hears such expressions as "Good morning," "Hello," "Hi," or "How ya doin?." Such greetings are sincere enough but something is missing. The rubric doesn't say "*Any* words of greeting may be used." It says "Any *apropriate* words --."

Someone has said that words, like eye glasses, blur anything that they do not make more clear. So with the word "PEACE." The biblical sense of "peace" is the positive meaning of the Hebrew word "Shalom," which was translated into the Greek "eirene," thence into the Latin "pax," which through Old French and Middle English "pais" became our "peace."

Both the Greek and Latin words were negative, denoting the absence or termination of war. But the root of "shalom" is "totality," "well-being," or "harmony." It expresses the ideal state of life in Israel. It appears 17 times in the Pentateuch alone, where its meaning includes material prosperity, good health, freedom from violence or misfortune, and every form of happiness which can occur in community with others. The prophets expanded the meaning, proclaiming that its source was Yahweh, and that its ultimate fulfillment would be either the rule of Israel's Messiah over all nations, or the paradisaic existence from which all strife has been removed. Jesus knew the word well, used it often, and added a dimension to it that his followers and then the Church completely accepted. At the Passover supper, after Judas had left the room, Jesus told the disciples that the Father would send the Holy Spirit, in Jesus's name, to teach them. Then he said: "Peace is my parting gift to your, my own peace, such as the world cannot give."

This then is the Peace which the Celebrant passes on to the congregation. This is the Peace which each member of the congregation may pass on, using "any appropriate words." The words "The Peace of the Lord (be with you)" may be the most appropriate words.

THE GENTLEMAN

Margaret B. Stegman Covenant Presbyterian Church
January, 1991

He was "dignity" personified
    with cropped white hair and suit of gray.
Sitting his chair as he would a steed
    he was wheeled down the long church aisle
to the pews where the family waited.
A grandson grinned his Welcome
    and reached for the old man's hand.
Granpere slumped, then straightened as
    a nurse in white and a daughter attentive
roused him when he dozed.
The sermon this morning was their tenderness
    - until the offering plate was passed
instead of putting his envelope in,
    (as a cookie from a tray of many,)
he quite delicately slipped one out.
The family returned the envelope
    along with his very own, but
so profound was the old man's innocence
    he shriveled inside his suit
without comprehension of what was wrong.

NOTES

1. This report was written by members of the G-3 Operations Section, 37th Infantry Div. Col. Russell A. Ramsey, as Chief of Staff, directed this operation as the forward element of the division command group. (R.W.R.)

2. One of these Silver Stars, and also the Purple Heart for wounds to the left arm and leg from an exploding Japanese mortar round, went to Col. Ramsey. (R.W.R.)

3. The speech was delivered at a community in southern Ohio. (R.W.R.)

4. General William Hull commanded U.S. forces in this campaign, which was a fiasco. When the War of 1812 ended, he was convicted for dereliction of duty. (R.W.R.)

5. General Ramsey referred here to his son, Russell W., who was a captain in command of an infantry company in the 1st Cavalry Division in Vietnam. (R.W.R.)

6. The editorial and material quoted came from an article in the *Gainsville* (Florida) *Sun* by General Ramsey's son, Major Russell W. Ramsey. (R.W.R.)

INDEX

Albany, GA 10, 71-74
Armed Forces Staff College 64
Baumeister 7, 30
Beightler, Claire 47
Beightler, Maj. Gen. 34-7, 45-8
Bougainville 36, 39
Brady 60, 67
Bricker 36
Buckingham 60
Camp Breckinridge 54-5
Camp Perry 31
Camp Shelby 31-2
Campbell School 7, 12, 30, 43, 61
Covenant Presbyterian Church 74
Denig 36
Didelius 47-9, 60
Eastern Airlines 48-9
83rd Reserve Div. 47-9, 51-5, 58
11th Airborne Division 40
Fiji Islands 36, 51
1st (Air) Cavalry Division 40-1, 60
Flynn 25
Ft. Benning 55, 60
Ft. Bragg 71-2
Ft. Campbell 55
Ft. Hayes 47
Ft. Knox 20-1
Ft. Leavenworth 37-9
Ft. Meade 58
Ft. Sill 20, 35

XIVth Army Corps 36, 40-1
Gainesville 61, 64, 66-73
Gilley 70
Good Samaritan Hospital 28, 49, 62, 66
Grace Episcopal Church 11-2, 24, 28, 45, 49-52, 61, 66, 73, 75
Graefe 59
Grizwald 36, 39, 41
Guerin 11
Hardy 52, 67, 72
Harten, Helen W. R. 11-19, 23-24, 26, 29, 35, 45-6, 69
Harten, Ted 29, 35, 45-6
Hartung 45, 49
Hattiesburg 31, 34-5, 55, 60
Holy Trinity Episcopal Church 66, 73, 75
Holzaphel 60
Houck, Beth 52, 67, 70
Houck, Dustin & Daniel 70
Houston, Archibald 6
Houston, Julia 6
Howe Military School 11-14, 53, 72, 76
Indian Town Gap 35-6
Kent State University 63-4
King 5, 11, 25
Liebenthal 59, 67, 71-2
Lind 59

Little 43
Louisiana 35
Luthman 74
MacArthur 37, 40-1
McNamara 57
McNelly 54
Michigan Law College 19-20, 22-3, 76
Morris 16, 18, 20, 26, 29, 35, 55, 76
Naples 46
Ohio State University 5, 15, 17-9, 23, 52-3, 61
Okamoto 45, 47
Patterson 28
Patton 35
Philippines 37, 39-45, 47, 60
Price, Sally 60, 67, 71
Price, Eric 71
Princeton University 15, 50, 52, 76
Pyle 11, 25
Ramsey, Ellen 55, 67
Ramsey, Florence 5-6, 8-9, 12, 26
Ramsey, Gustavus & Margaret 5
Ramsey, Linda 55, 60-1, 68
Ramsey, Lousie 9, 23-6, 28, 30-2, 34-7, 39, 43, 45-7, 50-2, 55-7, 59-60, 62, 64-73, 75
Ramsey, Norman 20
Ransey, Raymond 5, 9, 20
Ramsey, Robert 20
Ramsey, Roberta 69-70, 72, 74-5
Ramsey, Russell 70-73, 75
Ramsey, Russell K. 5-6, 8-16, 18-9, 24-6, 28, 49, 51-2, 76
Ramsey, Russell W. 31-2, 34, 37-9, 41, 43-6, 51-5, 57, 60-2, 64, 68, 72-3, 75
Ramsey, William 20
Reagan, 10, 71
Sandusky High School 13, 43, 50
Sikes 61-2
VIth U.S. Army 42
Smith, Carl 69

Smith, Jay 71
Smith, Randy 69
Smith, Susan 71
Smith, Robert & Lois 70
Solomon Islands 36-7, 39
Staunton Military Academy 53-4
Steinemann 11
Taylor 55
37th National Guard Division 7, 10, 13, 27-8, 30-2, 34-36, 39-45, 47, 61, 63-64, 71
University of Florida 61, 70
Van Dootingh 71
Waldock, Andrew 59, 67, 71-2
Waldock, Andy 71
Waldock, Becky 52, 60, 67
Waldock, Bill Jr. 52
Waldock, Bill Sr. & Ernestine 52, 59
Waldock, Florence 26-7, 30-2, 34, 37, 39, 43-6, 50, 52, 55, 59, 61-2, 72-3, 75-6
Waldock, Fred 52
Waldock, Jack Jr. 59, 67, 71
Waldock, Jill 71
Waldock, Johnny 71
Waldock, John 52, 55, 59-62
Wellesley College 51-2
Weichel 52
West Point 15, 17-8, 37, 52-5
Wilcox, Janet 9, 26, 29, 36
Wilcox, Lois 30
Wilcox, Merrit 9, 23, 26, 29-30, 36
Wilcox, Richard 9, 12, 23, 30
Williams, 11
Zuck 35